ESSENTIAL
PSYCHOLOGY

General Editor
Peter Herriot

C5

IN AND OUT
OF SCHOOL

ESSENTIAL

PSYCHOLOGY

IN AND OUT
OF SCHOOL

An introduction
to applied psychology
in education

Joan Freeman

Methuen

First published in 1975 by Methuen & Co Ltd
11 New Fetter Lane, London EC4P 4EE
© Joan Freeman 1975
Printed in Great Britain by
Richard Clay (The Chaucer Press), Ltd
Bungay, Suffolk
ISBN (hardback) 416 83740 9
ISBN (paperback) 416 83750 6

We are grateful to Grant McIntyre of Open
Books Ltd. for editorial assistance in the
preparation of this Series.

Contents

Editor's Introduction

Developmental psychologists tell us something about the ways in which people grow as individuals. Education involves in some sense participating, assisting, or intervening in this process of development; it seems to follow that educators should find the psychologist's theories and findings of considerable help. Unfortunately the relationship isn't so straightforward as it first appears. We are a long way from discovering how maturation and experience, nature and nurture, interact. Therefore it is difficult to know which experiences to provide, when to provide them, and how to present them. Our ignorance of child development is a scientific misfortune; education is also the product of attitudes and values. It is constrained by social and economic factors, so educators may be able to take account only of the psychological factors involved. Joan Freeman picks a delicate path through this minefield. She concentrates on the *practical* uses to which psychological concepts and skills have been put, and her book is essential reading for anyone who intends to be involved in education.

This book belongs to Unit C of *Essential Psychology*. What unifies the titles in this unit is the concept of development. It is a very rich concept, embodying as it does the notions of process and change, and the interaction of a human being with his environment throughout his life. The individual has to maintain some sort of equilibrium between the demands of the environment and his own way of constructing reality. He has to adapt to the realities of the particular culture he lives in; but at the same time, he may be able to change his environment to a certain extent. In this way, equilibrium may be maintained without compromising his own conceptual system. The concept of development is thus ideal for dealing with growing up and changing in society. We can use the phrase 'personal development' to talk both about children and about adults; this may help us to see both as people. The reader will find other conceptual frameworks in other units. They are not so much mutually contradictory as efforts to do justice to the complexities of psychology's subject matter. Coming to terms with a variety of explanatory frameworks decreases our confidence in psychology as a mature science; but perhaps it is better to be honest about what we don't know.

Essential Psychology as a whole is designed to reflect the changing structure and function of psychology. The authors are both academics and professionals, and their aim has been to introduce the most important concepts in their areas to beginning students. They have tried to do so clearly but have not attempted to conceal the fact that concepts that now appear central to their work may soon be peripheral. In other words, they have presented psychology as a developing set of views of man, not as a body of received truth. Readers are not intended to study the whole series in order to 'master the basics'. Rather, since different people may wish to use different theoretical frameworks for their own purposes, the series has been designed so that each title stands on its own. But it is possible that if the reader has read no psychology before, he will enjoy individual books more if he has read the introductions (A1, B1, etc.) to the units to which they belong. Readers of the units concerned with applications of psychology (E,F) may benefit from reading all the introductions.

A word about references in the text to the work of other writers – e.g. 'Smith, 1974'. These occur where the author feels he must acknowledge an important concept or some crucial evidence by name. The book or article referred to will be listed in the references (which double as name index) at the back of the book. The reader is invited to consult these sources if he wishes to explore topics further. A list of general further reading is also to be found at the back of the book.

We hope you enjoy psychology.   *Peter Herriot*

Introduction

The value of psychology in education is in providing a basis for decisions – when to intervene, and when to step aside in guiding a child's progress along his own educational route. Educational practice is founded on the educator's personal understanding of the range of normal development processes in children (see C1 of *Essential Psychology*); it is both a science and an art. To educate well calls upon every resource the educator can muster, as well as a wide open mind ready to learn and relearn the business of education.

Learning begins even before birth. As yet, education, in the sense of positive intervention by another, is only available from then on. Natural development or maturation, both physical and intellectual, can be changed from the basic inherited plan. Nothing in life is fixed and immutable. A knowledge of development implies that we expect certain changes to happen within a particular range of time in a child's life. If such changes are not within the range of what might be expected, then there may be cause for suspicion that something may be amiss, and some action to be taken.

Judgement and action based on knowledge imply some form of assessment. Intuitive feelings are not to be undervalued. They may bring about an essential preliminary check, using whatever information sources are available, leading perhaps to professional help. But the clearest diagnosis and the most effective help stem from expertise rather than 'feelings'. The true educator, either parent or teacher, already has a considerable amount of information available, but obviously the use made of it varies to extremes.

Education is understood in this book in its broadest sense. To educate is to alter behaviour in some way – whether that behaviour is thinking or doing. Educators generally assume that their intervention is beneficial to the child, though there is some disagreement on that point. What is sure is that a child cannot grow and learn without material to feed on. Whatever a child receives can only be a tiny, and largely pre-selected, portion of possible life experience, in which chance plays a large part.

We do have guidelines to the developmental processes through which most children pass. We also have considerable evidence of the most facilitating conditions in which children might thrive. Although no power on earth can endow every new-born with stability and wide educational opportunity, ordinary mortals are becoming continually better equipped to help children to help themselves to what is actually available.

It is the aim of this short book to pick out some of the many aspects of developmental psychology as they might be applied to education, in the hope that educators and children both might use them to advantage. Psychology can be applied in education in the following general way: it can suggest some research-based concepts which might be useful to teachers. Teachers may change their general attitudes towards teaching and their overall strategies, and they may adopt certain specific methods or techniques.

Part One
EDUCATION OUT OF SCHOOL

Education as a changing process and the psychological
conditions which affect it

I
Children's Abilities

Major influences

All children have abilities; even the most severely handicapped can learn to respond to the rattle of the food trolley. But performance at any level is restricted by the two major boundaries of what is available both in terms of mental equipment and of educational opportunities, i.e. of heredity and environment.

Considerable information has accumulated on children's abilities at different ages (at least in the West), which provides a useful guide on what performance to expect. Although a spot comparison with other children's performances will tell us if a child is slow for his age, it will not tell us his individual pattern of development, or that his parents have just been divorced or that he'll catch up later.

What we can be sure of is that genes carry potential abilities and that these are inherited at conception. Genetic inheritance defines the limits of any effect that the enviroment could possibly have. Children cannot be made to perform more ably than they are capable of doing, but of course they can perform less well than that. It is the proportion of the effects of heredity and environment that are of particular concern to education. Some psychologists such as Eysenck (1971) and Jensen (1972) have concluded from research results that heredity is responsible for about 80 per cent of our potential –

which only leaves about 20 per cent to work on. They reason that, because of this fixed potential, children should be sorted into educational groups at an early age and given a form of education which is considered to be most suitable for their abilities (see D3).

Both Eysenck and Jensen are now particularly well known for their emotive association of race with ability, focusing on intelligence. Both the concepts of race and of ability are defined and measured by the methods available at this time (which may need improvement). The statistical results have been followed by reasoned argument but they are, of course, open to other equally valid interpretations and conclusions. However, because of the emotional accompaniment, the basic assumption in the argument that separating children out and giving them special education is beneficial, has been twisted out of recognition. It was, after all, a similar argument which brought about the selection of secondary school children in 1944 – that each child should be educated according to ability.

The appearance of outstanding individuals in families of low cultural level has always been unexpected; Bunyan, for example, was the son of a tinker. If mental abilities (in so far as they are innate) are transmitted in the same manner as physical characteristics, then in biological terms such anomalies would be expected from time to time. Even so, it is not yet possible to predict when these spontaneous mutations will occur, although one out of every five children carry a new mutation inherited from one of the parents.

As so little is still known about the proportion of inherited ability, it is possible to consider that perhaps there is no fixed ratio and that some children inherit a greater proportion than others. If we could be certain that 80 per cent of ability is innate, and that we could measure it accurately, it would make sense to start each child off on an educational programme from which he or she could derive most benefit. For instance, should innate ability in music prove to be of overriding importance, then the primary school hours spent on recorder teaching might be irrelevant, if not irritating (and so counter-productive), to many children. But if appreciation and performing ability are largely the products of environment, then perhaps there should be a more generous spread of musical opportunity. Since intelligence tests do not measure innate and fixed ability, and probably will never be able to in principle, let alone in practice, these speculations are fruitless.

In our present state of confusion, it would seem unjust to deny all-round educational opportunity to any child, particularly of primary school age. The swings of educational policy are not necessarily based on the relative logic of research reports; the political climate of the time and perhaps a pinch of faith in the environmental 'cause' is slowly moving the State educational system towards non-selection. But real equality of educational opportunity is another matter.

selective ed.

Some theories

The nature and structures of human abilities have exercised the minds of psychologists for over a century and of philosophers long before then. One approach is to view abilities as relatively unchanging characteristics of the individual. The results of intelligence tests are used to try to discover which are the different abilities involved. Essentially, the questions on the intelligence are separated into groups; the basis of separating a group of questions is that if a person gets one right, he is likely to get the other ones from the group right also. The group of questions is arrived at by a statistical technique known as factor analysis.

In 1904, Spearman outlined his simple, elegant theory of intelligence, known as the two-factor theory. A general ability factor called 'g' was considered as fixed; specific ability factors called 's' were open to environmental influence. Even today, psychologists can be overheard to describe children in terms of 'g'.

Thurstone, in the mid-twenties, refined the statistics and testing further and produced a model with seven 'primary' abilities. This was the first attempt to provide a profile of ability. But the 'primary' abilities were found to overlap and his tests were no more accurate predictors than any others.

The work of Burt (1940) in England largely contributed to the notion of a hierarchical structure of ability. According to Burt, a single general ability factor is related to a variety of lesser factors, and these in their turn subsume more specific ability factors.

to include under a class as belonging to it

15

But there are limitations to the factor approach:

1 Interpretation of the factors is always subjective.
2 Resultant factors always depend on the means used to gather the data.
3 Labelling a factor as an ability is a result of subjective interpretation; a statistical result does not imply a psychological process.

The above theories and models are not now regarded as worthless because of these limitations, but rather as mathematical concepts which fail to do justice to the richness and variety of potential ability. Guilford (1967) puts forward a more complicated and seminal model of the intellect. The basic features of this model are: the type of content (e.g. words, number); the mental operation performed (e.g. deductive reasoning); and the nature of the end-product of the mental operations (e.g. a conclusion). Guilford has described 120 distinguishable abilities, by combining these types of feature in every possible way; thus one ability for example would be the ability to perform deductive reasoning upon sentences presented auditorily and produce the necessary logical conclusion.

Like Guilford, Cattell (1965) broadened the scope of traditional intelligence tests. He, too, set problems which did not require the testee to arrive at an answer which the psychologist had already decided was the right one. In addition to the familiar deductive and inductive reasoning tests, then, Cattell included questions to which there was no correct answer, but which sought to test the ability to answer in a novel way. He realised, further, that such abilities depended to a large extent on personality characteristics; for example, strongly authoritarian people tend to feel that there can only be one correct answer.

Piaget (see C1, C2) rejects the types of theory, outlined above, where mental activities can be lined up and ordered into static models or patterns. His view of intellectual activity is based on the biological principle of balance, or homeostasis. That is, the child has to keep in balance the demands of the environment and his own ways of thinking about it. He is an active participant in building his own intelligence, constantly constructing his reality rather than merely detecting information. Indeed, according to Piaget, actually manipulating one's

16

environment is a necessary precondition to any form of symbolic thinking.

It is Piaget's influence which is largely responsible for changing the style of education of many primary schools. Although he is not the only educationalist to insist on the child's being active in the learning situation, he has brought about the concept and practice of 'child-centred', as opposed to the older 'teacher-centred' education. The other theories mentioned above have had relatively little effect on educational practice, as they stand, but have exerted their influence on the psychologist's approach to the investigation of intelligence, particularly in the formation of intelligence tests.

Perceptual learning (see C3 and C4)

The human being is neither a tape-recorder nor a movie-camera. The events in the outside world which he sees or hears are not perceived in their literal, physical form. On the contrary, the brain makes sense of information, transforming it into a coded version. Adults have well-learned codes which enable them to perceive reality in this way. For example, we can judge the distance ahead of a car by using the cues of perspective.

How does the child acquire these codes? He starts by co-ordinating the impressions he receives from the different senses. For example he learns to coordinate touch and sight so that he can grasp and manipulate an object he can see. Experience of this sort enables the child to transform his sense impressions into more abstract, or symbolic representations of objects and events. These representations may contain certain features of objects which he has abstracted: for example, the roundness of a ball and its kickability. Hence he can come to make fine discriminations between something round and something not quite round, since roundness is a feature with which he is familiar. The ease with which he discriminates will be increased by various factors. For example, the language of others will encourage him to pay particular attention to certain features of his environment by naming them. Further, a child may be rewarded for making certain discriminations successfully – to distinguish mummy and daddy and call them by their names is thoroughly rewarding all round.

17

Conceptual development (see C2)

The child's intellectual development can, then, be described in terms of the degree of abstraction employed in his perception. It is, indeed, important to realise that he ceases to code objects in terms of their surface characteristics, such as their colour, and starts to look at them in terms of their function (e.g. the fact that they are all items of clothing). But it is of yet greater importance to note the changes in the complexity of the mental operations he can perform upon these codings. For example, by around 6–8 he can probably reverse a mental operation – he knows not only that $2+2=4$, but also that $4-2=2$. Or he can see a class of objects as being subordinate to another class (e.g. roses are flowers) and also the superordinate class as subsuming smaller classes (e.g. some flowers are roses). Of course, the two sorts of development are related; it is much easier to perform more complex operations when using more abstract symbols. The child cannot see that a sausage-shaped piece of plasticine can be rolled back again into the round ball it once was if he is concentrating on the actual length of the sausage. He needs to be able to conceptualise the quantity of plasticine as remaining the same, regardless of its current shape.

The development of the child's thinking follows a series of stages of complexity in the mental operations he can perform. Each is a necessary precondition of the next. Therefore it is of vital importance that the child engages in the sort of experience appropriate to his stage of development.

If he lacks this experience, the whole of his subsequent development will suffer. Therefore, the perceptual learning of the child in his early years must be the major concern of the teacher. How can she direct the child's attention to the important features of his environment?

Attention in the classroom

Already we start attacking a practical problem. Here are some generalisations about attention which the teacher may find useful.

1 Change attracts attention. Were many a lecturer to stop read-

18

ing his notes suddenly, he would acquire the attention of the whole class. Clapping hands is frequently used by teachers to change the classroom noise and draw attention.

2 Contrast is not quite the same as change, referring to something which stands out from the background. It is particularly useful in display, in a child's bedroom, or the classroom.

3 Repetition, as every teacher knows, is a part of teaching. A weak stimulus repeated several times can be more effective than a strong one given only once. But here lies the art; too much repetition leads to boredom or worse. Although one hand-clap may be insufficient and three claps draw attention, twenty claps might bring in next-door's children.

4 Intensity is an effective attention device. Loud sounds dominate lower sounds, big pictures catch attention before small ones. But continual shouting at children is known to lose its original intensive effect.

5 Novelty contributes to attention and recall. How often are the anecdotes remembered, when the lecture is long forgotten.

6 Social suggestion is following the actions of a group, such as the old game children play of staring into a tree until a crowd gathers. Children working together on a theme can increase each other's attention this way.

Distraction is the drawing away of attention, and in the educational context raises many questions. What causes the failure of attention? How is the educational material being presented? How easily does a particular child become distracted? How costly in energy are distracting, say noisy, conditions?

Perceptual set. When a child is attending to a particular sort of event in his environment or in his mind, this enables him to prepare in advance for various demands that may be made upon him. He may start selecting ahead which sort of strategy will be appropriate. This is why psychologists always give children a trial run on each type of task in a psychological test. If children all turn up for a history lesson and find it has changed to biology, they will have to make a considerable mental adjustment.

Creativity

We have so far been dealing with the stages of cognitive development, which characterise all children; we have just looked at ways of developing children's attention so that their development may be facilitated. But what of those children who react in unusually creative ways to the learning situation? High scores on creativity tests are viewed with suspicion by teachers, who prefer to choose their exceptionally creative children themselves. Educators accept an unusual vocabulary, imaginative writing, unusual and original behaviour as indicators of giftedness. But it seems very probable that the child with mechanical gifts will remain unidentified. Teacher assessment is always tricky due to the bias of the teacher's own personality, background and attitudes; parental assessment has even less to recommend it. And yet intuitive feelings have their honoured place in identifying and assessing, but preferably along with other methods.

Creative ability itself is the most difficult to pin down. What is tested as creative has considerable overlap with many other abilities. Indeed the IQ may be the best single criterion for creative potential, even as it stands. But measuring any creative activity, while disregarding emotion and personality, is the sort of sterile psychological exercise which creative people complain of. Research work on creative personalities using Cattell's 16 PF test found that creative people were stable, careless of other's opinions, and somewhat anxious. Other researchers have included interest ratings. But all the present tests of creativity are expected to be completed in a short space of time. It is unlikely that creative endeavour can always be turned on at the examiner's convenience. Originality may need developed concern over time, maybe even years to mature. The time aspect of creativity has not come under investigation yet.

Most of the experimental work on creativity has been visual, but attempts are being made to investigate auditory (i.e. musical) creativity. Some creativity may be related to intelligence and some not. It is only possible to say that whereas high IQ does not guarantee high creativity, low IQ certainly militates against it.

Children's abilities are to some extent flexible and alterable. It is in the manoeuvrings of their educational worlds, both in and out of school, that abilities take on forms which will, to a large extent, stay that way through life.

important
could use — ed/essay

2
Intellectual and Physical Development

Maturation implies an inherent, preordained 'unfolding' of potential, which is already there. Growth involves gain of some sort and is a part of maturation. Both are part of development, which we may see as the changes which occur as the result of the maturing child's interaction with his environment. It is essential in the practice of education to know the normal pattern of children's development, but on the understanding that what is normal is only an average – to be used as a comparison when measuring an individual's development – rather than an absolute measure.

There can be great differences between children of the same age, and between the developmental rates of different abilities in one child. Every child has his or her own individual tempo and style in growth, as personal as a facial outline. Human development occurs in fits and starts, with pauses in between. Even the norms change yearly, as children mature earlier; and this itself varies between cultures. To get the best response from teaching, it would be ideal for an educator to know exactly where each child is in terms of his development of any particular ability. An impossible task!

All development in children is contained by two boundaries:

1 Genetic inheritance.
2 Nourishment – both mental and physical.

The current developmental level of the child will limit his educational achievement. If the task requires mental operations of which he's not yet capable, he will, of course, fail. He may, nevertheless, sometimes 'get the right answer' by other means – for example by learning by rote. But another cause of failure may be that the child has had his present potential limited by his previous inadequate experience when at an earlier stage of development. This is why it is so important to tackle and remedy the cycle of deprivation early in a child's life. This applies to both mental and physical growth, which are considered together in this chapter as different but inseparable aspects of an individual.

Infancy

Behaviour starts in a four-week old foetus when the heart begins to beat. By the time a baby is born, it has quite a complicated range of well-practised movements and its own individual ways of carrying out life processes, breathing, feeding, reacting, etc. Gesell (1950) stresses the organising processes of growth and the contexts in which it takes place. Even from conception, this is important. Various common drugs, such as nicotine and aspirin, affect development. Nourishment, the mother's age, and stress can, for example, affect the progress of pregnancy. Prematurely born babies are less likely to fare well in many ways.

A child alters through growth, different aspects affecting each other. That first step, for instance, enables a vast expanse of life to be sampled, from touching and tasting, to being able to actively seek affection when it is needed. The baby's social and personal image is also changed. By the age of a year, an infant has developed at a rate which it will never reach again. But the processes and personal style of its growth will remain essentially the same throughout life. Each infant learns in his own way, changing behaviour by trial and error, though always with reference to his available ability.

But from the beginning, the urge to learn is tempered by opportunity. The responses of even tiny babies to shapes and noises can be related to the type of care they have received. A mother's handling of her baby is in many ways indicative of her own upbringing and how it is passed on, but the baby's response to it is also important. Girl babies seem to have more sensitive skins than boy babies; heavy babies respond differently from wiry babies. The effects of emotional deprivation were published by Bowlby (1951), in his summary of studies around the world, based on institutionalised infants. Although he later seemed to reach an extreme view on the dire effects of mother–child separation, the point was made. Emotional deprivation is psychologically crippling and it can occur in any level of society. Later studies, especially those of Harlow (1959) with monkeys, have shown how behaviour patterns are learned and passed on over generations (see Part Three).

Intellectual development

In the growth of psychological understanding (outlined on p. 15) it can be seen that narrow and often misleading definitions of intelligence are giving way to the idea of a relatively flexible intellect, which can only be described in terms of a 'profile'; one number is scarcely sufficient. Intelligence itself is regarded more as a way of behaving, which can be developed. Aspects of intelligence such as reasoning or learning ability are recognised as owing much to past experience, i.e. what has already been learned, especially in the early years. Intelligence tests are increasingly regarded as a type of achievement test and as such, good predictors of future achievement in school work. They are useful tools in education, but need skilled handling, like any other tools (see Chapter 8).

All intellectual growth (covered in C1 and C2) is important in education. The following, generally accepted, major developments are particularly so:

Symbolic behaviour. This includes language (see A7), learning and thinking, which are considered to be interdependent. At the age of about a year, an infant is normally well advanced. He listens and responds to words and signs, will have learned to produce a few, and practises with babble. He can put one cube after another on the table – the basis of counting. He responds to music.

Symbolic behaviour is the clearest indicator of educational growth, and language, in particular vocabulary, is the most easily measurable of these indicators. Individuals vary greatly in early language acquisition, and this is not a reliable guide to their future intellectual ability. Learning to speak, read and write is affected by a number of factors such as emotional security and need for communication by that particular route.

As words are learned they carry with them overtones of the emotional situation in which they were learned. These 'feelings' attached to words can change as the experiences associated with the words change. Few words are free of emotional overtones, language is both informative and emotional.

The rate and breadth of children's language is directly related to the language behaviour of the adults who look after them. Language is learned by feedback – being heard, corrected, using words to control, etc. Underprivileged children often lack this necessary feedback. The middle-class child improves his language ability with parental intervention, the working-class child has to depend more on its effect. Thus a difference in communication styles grows and some children need help more than others. Developing spontaneous speech in children who are not used to speaking is extremely difficult. Methods which are successful with middle-class children are usually doomed to failure, as children with poor speech are usually poor in perceptual and other abilities too.

Bernstein's theory (1960) of the social-class structuring of language codes found immediate sympathy in his readers before there was any respectable evidence for it. In this, he proposes two codes of speech; the 'elaborated' code, used by the middle classes, and the simple 'restricted' code, used by the working classes and children together. As language is tied up with thinking, working-class children are supposedly restricted by their culture in their ability to communicate with the middle-class world such as teachers and schools, and so are handicapped in their academic achievement.

There are also the variety of children in British schools who have not learned English as their native tongue. Girls have been found to be more verbally able than boys, whereas boys score more highly in mathematics. Although the social influences on these symbolic behaviours is difficult to gauge, parents and teachers who are aware can try to counterbalance them and release potential in both girls and boys (see Chapter 6).

Time sense. As children develop, they are increasingly able to juggle with time. Memory is helped by an increasing use of language as a shorthand for concepts and by the reinforcement of experience in perception and understanding. Planning becomes consistently easier.

Reasoning. Perception affects reasoning too; where experience is lacking, good reasoning based on mistaken perceptions brings about faulty conclusions. In a persistent child, this can be damaging to intellectual growth. Education is largely concerned with correcting mis-perception by broadening the view, so that a child can reach his own conclusions from these new experiences.

The most abstract and difficult thought normally comes within reach about the mid-teens, if at all. There is thus little point in discussing abstruse ideas with primary school children. But ideas based on real experiences, especially their own, will most often make contact with lively young minds.

Learning to read

Making sense out of visual symbols is a vital part of language development and communication. Many people leave school never having acquired the ability to read – a social and intellectual disablement, which is unlikely to be due to any deficiency in the individual. Given enough time and suitable help, all normal children should be able to read. However, the roots of reading ability go deep, involving the following influences.

Language development. In order to read, a child must first have sufficient command of words. (See above p. 23) Familiarity with words, how they are used, and how they are combined (see A6 Chapter 7) is a part of recognising what is presented on paper. Sources of language-confusion in the early stages of reading can be:

1 having to read and memorise unfamiliar words.
2 dialect variations, particularly in vowel sounds, so that the spoken word does not match what is written.
3 speech handicaps, such as lisping or stuttering, which may need the help of a speech therapist.

Parents or teachers who are aware of the child's problem(s) can help by enriching the child's language. This can be done by providing experiences such as day trips, or activities in the home or classroom which can be talked about afterwards. Constructive listening, as described by Joan Tough (1973), and as practical in normal educationally supportive homes, is a vital preliminary to reading.

Perception. Self-perception has a considerable effect on all learning. Feelings of unworthiness are always detrimental. Poor physical development such as weakness or clumsiness can, for instance, lower a child's view of himself and his confidence to read. Extreme sensitivity, self-consciousness and lack of friends are also associated with poor reading.

Faults in vision and hearing are usually detected before a child reaches school, but some children slip through the net. Teachers should be aware of this possibility. Minor perceptual difficulties are no obstacle to reading if they are detected early on. Major perceptual difficulties such as the inability to distinguish letters are considered in Chapter 11. Reading English involves a left to right, line by line progression, which has particular problems for left handed children.

Auditory perception is the sole method of language learning in infancy. Some children can be deaf in certain tonal ranges, and constant bouts of catarrh can produce temporary hearing deficiencies which inhibit language learning. Teaching reading by the phonic method means that a child must be able to split words up into sounds; his auditory discrimination must therefore be sufficient for the process. Word games and discrimination exercises are of help.

Memory. Reading is very dependent on visual memory. Individual words and letters must be recognised and reproducible, often in different forms. Letters are learned as capitals, small letters, joined-up writing, different forms of printing, typing, etc. Frequent repetition is a memory aid; but too much harping on the same theme can have an adverse effect. Children can remember words better which have more meaning for them, or which they like the sound of. Memory games and activities can be devised to make the learning easier, more meaningful and longer lasting.

Environment. Poor environment, as described in Chapter 11, has a depressing effect on both the starting age and the extent of reading ability. A child's language range and usage, his attitudes to the written word, and to the world of school are well formed before the age of five. Research into poor reading consistently finds that lack of books in the home, mothers who work all day, large families, lack of parental interest, poor health, etc., are all detrimental. Schools can, and do, succeed in supplementing poor home background, although strongly conflicting demands of home and school may be distressing and so counterproductive. Children in such a situation may mentally or physically 'drop out of learning, at a tender age.

Motivation. As with all learning – success breeds success. Strong motivation goes a long way to make up for limited capacity. Negative feelings can bring reading to a full stop. First reading experiences should always be successful and exciting. Later reading can be reinforced by talking about what has been read, acting, art work, films, visits and the tremendously useful tape-recorder. This last is a most useful device, by which not only can the child improve his language skills, but the teacher too can discover her own use of language in teaching.

Intrinsic motivation can only begin to develop when the child understands the importance and purpose of reading and writing. This begins with being read to, at home and at school.

Reading readiness. This is a concept which has deprived children of reading tuition and frightened parents into witholding reading help until a child is of an 'official' age to begin. It has been especially prevalent in America. We now accept that it is probably more harmful to a child to delay reading, and so lose his valuable enthusiasm. Current concern is with finding the appropriate method to suit the individual. Children do seem to develop their own strategies to a large extent. The sensitive educator takes her clues on readiness and progress from the child's sensory and intellectual development. Readiness is a matter of being able to meet the demands of the task, and to relate it to previous learning. The intellectual skills needed can be recognised in a child's ability to:

1 follow oral instructions

2 retell the main points in a story, in correct sequence
3 describe pictures in some detail
4 anticipate what will happen
5 describe what he has done and heard.

Does the child show interest in trying to read signs or advertisements; to construct and use complete sentences, to play with sounds and words? Efficient reading necessitates keeping a whole word or phrase in mind, while attention is paid to parts of the word or phrase.

As a basis for reading, a child should have a vocabulary of about two hundred words. An ability to discriminate between sounds in sequence, and to blend them smoothly and rhythmically into words should be apparent, before teaching to read phonetically can succeed.

Reading and writing go together. Writing acts as a kind of physical reinforcement of the breaking up of words into their different sounds, and the reblending process, which puts the sense back. The physical component of writing does, however, add some extra difficulties to its learning processes, which are similar to those of reading.

Teaching reading. There are many reading schemes on the market today. Their relative merits are not discussed here.

Reading is dependent on development processes. It should be taught in relation to speaking, listening and writing. The chosen reading scheme should be relevant to the interests of the individual child; ideally varying between children. Reading material should be well illustrated and clearly printed in large letters. As the scheme progresses, so should the variation in type of story and breadth of interest. Supplementary reading should also be carefully chosen to complement the scheme.

Physical development

There is reasonable cause to believe, from physiological research reports, that intellectual growth cannot take place until the appropriate physical growth in the nervous system is complete. Voluntary behaviour takes place by courtesy of the central nervous system, which includes the brain. Messages are transmitted by nerve cells (called neurones), which throw the information from one cell to another across a gap or synapse. The more frequently the route across that synapse is used, the easier the jump becomes. This facilitation of the synapse forms the basis of learning and habit, but it cannot take place until physical maturation allows it to. 'There is also plenty of evidence that, in the brain, functions appear when structures mature, and not before' (Tanner 1968).

Maturation. The dependence of mental abilities on maturational changes in the brain applies to all levels of thought, even the highest. It is recognised by Piaget and Inhelder, along with the need for a suitable social environment. Maturational processes in humans such as standing up, or sphincter control, appear to take place without the need of teaching. The greatest interference with maturation is probably starvation which, whilst preventing body growth, also prevents intellectual growth. The duration of starvation and the stage of development involved will affect the total outcome. Other interferences are genetic disorders, poisons, diseases, or physical damage.

Fig. 2.1 Growth curves
(Reproduced by kind permission of Blackwell Scientific Publications)

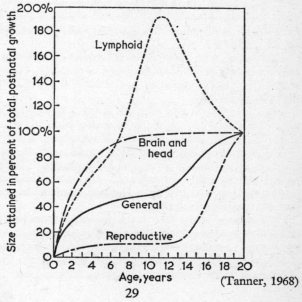

(Tanner, 1968)

Just as children vary enormously in their obvious physical maturation, they vary equally in brain maturation. The graph above is drawn from the combined results of thousands of children and may be used as a basis for comparison. It shows the variety of maturational patterns of just four major types of body growth.

The growth curves of intelligence, as measured by intelligence tests, are very similar to the curve of brain and head growth. Intelligence is not a fixed quantity, but can vary up or down over the years. Social and personality factors influence intelligence test scores, along with neurological maturation.

Emotional implications

Until puberty, obvious changes of size in boys and girls are much the same. New shoes for bigger feet are part of the pleasure of normal growing up. But after puberty, the change towards an adult shape and the surge of hormones becomes noticeable. The sudden increase in strength and size can cause clumsiness and embarrassment. Generally, all the pubertal and adolescent changes take place together, so that if a boy is a late maturer, he is late in all respects and that has probably been his life pattern.

Looking at, say, twelve-year-old girls or fourteen-year-old boys, it is easy to see their variation in maturity, even though their chronological ages may be the same. Emotional maturity tends to follow suit.

Growth of height and strength is particularly important to boys in Western society. Early maturing boys are able to become dominant and remain so. Alternatively, a boy's self-concept is lowered if body growth is considered to be poor, and this can reflect badly on school achievement. The psychological vicious circle impinges on boy/parent relationships, leading to longer dependence. But late maturing boys are apt to make more sensitive men.

Girls appear to be less psychologically disturbed by the changes of adolescence. Perhaps, as Tanner suggests, it is because they are actually 'older' already, i.e. further along the developmental road. However, school marks begin to suffer, particularly as the external social pressures build up.

Extreme rates of maturation are inevitably difficult for a child, but the effects are considerably cushioned by the support of a loving and secure family relationship. The underdeveloped boy will find acceptance at home and avoid the not uncommon feelings of rejection.

Educational implications

Bigger children are likely to be more able than smaller children of the same age. They will pass exams better, including school selection exams. Slower maturing children are at a disadvantage in a competitive school situation, regardless of their potential. Yet even when allowance is made for exact chronological age, nothing is allowed for developmental age. This applies to intelligence tests too. By the completion of growth, the late maturer will probably have caught up, but this will be too late as far as school and maybe future opportunities are concerned.

Ability tests, including intelligence tests, are always cross-sectional, comparing one child with the average for his age at a specific time. Children's individual style and progress over time are ignored in almost all testing, in spite of the evidence available. At very least, the school doctor's report can be a valuable asset in knowledgeable hands. Any scores should be considered in terms of individual development.

There is a tendency, particularly in primary schools, but also in secondary schools, to group children by ability for teaching. As long as these groups remain open and flexible, they may avoid the pitfalls of the formal classroom. In primary schools, some even spill over chronological age boundaries, so that differences in speed of growth in individuals can be catered for in the normal school.

3
Learning

The process of learning has been described in many different ways. We have stressed in this book so far the views of developmental psychologists. They conceive of learning as the adaptation of the child to new experience. That is, the child achieves a new state of equilibrium between his ways of thinking and the demands of the environment. Clearly, then, the nature and extent of the child's learning is dependent on the stage of cognitive development he has reached.

There are other views concerning the process of learning (see A3). One view stresses the importance of the consequences of behaviour. It suggests that when a piece of behaviour is followed by a reinforcement, that behaviour is more likely to occur in the future. We can think of a reinforcement as a reward, provided we realise that different events are rewarding to different people. (A public word of praise from a teacher might be a punishment, not a reward, for an adolescent.) This approach appears at first sight to require that the child is already practising the required behaviour, and that reinforcement only makes it appear more frequently. However, this is not so. Behaviour which only remotely resembles the desired behaviour may be refined down, or shaped, to the specific behaviour required. This is done by reinforcing only closer and closer approximations to the desired behaviour.

There are other theories of learning. The teacher will realise that all are very limited. For example, the operant conditional theory of Skinner described above shows how we may change people's behaviour. It does not describe how we may develop the mental operations which underlie intelligent behaviour. Nor does it for a moment explain why children behave as they do at a given point in time; this is a function of the continuous interaction of heredity and environment. On the other hand it may point to the need to specify what sort of behaviour is evidence that learning has taken place; and the need to praise good performance and give feedback as to success or failure. In other words, psychological theories of learning may each have something to offer, but all be sadly lacking if used as blueprints for educational practice. There follow, therefore, some features common to various learning theories which seem to be relevant to teachers.

The roots of learning

Motivation. This is perhaps the cornerstone of learning, implying a goal to be sought. Humans have very few needs to act as stimuli for motivation and even those are questionable, except the biological ones. Motivated behaviour towards a goal, even in children, is based on a complex mixture of expectation, social pressure, curiosity, reward, etc. With adulthood, needs become even more synthetic so that symbols such as high status or riches can become the goal. (see D2)

Motivation involves both 'need' in whatever sense, and self-concept. It requires energy to be spent in the search for a goal. It also implies a response to the success or failure of the operation.

Response. Learning cannot take place without the active participation or response of a child. The possible responses will, however, be limited by:

1 The level of maturation, or ability
2 Previous learning
3 Perception of the learning situation.

Responses to a learning situation will vary with the make-up of the individual. For example, success will be reinforcing, but it may also bring about disillusion or boredom if the goal was

33

set too low. Failure may bring about increased effort – a small obstacle in the way can produce this result – or it may result in despondency.

Generalisation is a process whereby new learning finds its way into other situations, which are not necessarily related.

Transfer is a more specific use of learning in an appropriate setting. It can be taught in situations which are similar, say two calculations in physics. It would be an essential part of that physics teaching to aid the transfer process, so that similar responses are seen to be needed in both calculations. This perception by the student of the similarities between problems and responses is essential to learning from the situation.

Negative transfer happens when something previously learned gets in the way of new learning. Changing from one make of car to another can be dangerous. The old brake is sought for, before the realisation that it's not there sets the driver searching for the new brake's position. The process of learning the new brake's position will take longer than the learning on the first car because some unlearning has to take place at the same time.

Habit. When learned behaviour becomes so entrenched that it becomes automatic, it is called a habit. Such habits dominate most of an adult's daily behaviour. They are constantly reinforced, as they are the 'easiest' form of behaviour. Breaking a habit is difficult because of the reinforcement and because of the complexity of causes which brought it about. Even stronger motivation is needed to change a habit.

Learning curves. The precise progress of learning can be plotted on to graphs. Learning can progress in a fairly smooth line or in fits and starts, depending on what is to be learned and how it has been taught.

A good teacher will know the behaviour of the learning curve and can offer knowledge and encouragement to the learner where effort seems to be getting less result.

Remembering. Retention of new learning depends very much on what happens after the learning, e.g. on the nature of the

34

interfering stimuli and on how close they are in time and similarity to the learning. For instance, we forget less during sleep than during waking hours. Remembering also depends on the degree to which we have operated on, or coded, the information. If we have integrated it with our established ways of thinking, we will remember it better.

Remembering is a selective process. Things forgotten may be offensive or boring. Taken to an extreme, this emotional aspect of forgetting becomes repression. Remembering is also likely to be distorted for the same reasons. When a task is completed, such as passing a final exam, the learning involved may be largely forgotten unless it is to be used soon. An unfinished task has a hangover; it becomes more easily remembered. Lesson: leave a task unfinished at the end of the day if you want to continue with it. Restarting mental activity the following day will be quicker.

Fig. 3.1 A learning plateau

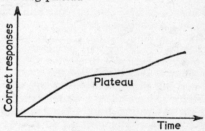

Measuring retention is important to an educator. Three simple methods are available:

1 Recall. The child is asked to repeat what he has learned; the most frequent method used. Exact reproduction, may be required.
2 Recognition. This is easier than recall, but nonetheless valuable. Multiple choice examinations work on this principle. Exact reproduction is not required, merely familiarity and identification.
3 Learning traces. When there is no obvious evidence that learning has taken place but relearning takes place much more quickly than could be expected, the traces of the first learning must have been retained. Recall and recognition may well miss these traces, which, although minimal, are still valuable in the learning process.

All the concepts we have mentioned above may be useful. But what more specific implications do they have for classroom teaching and for parents?

Assisted learning

1 *Encouraging motivation.* Adequate motivation for learning is initially present in all children. If it is absent or overpowering, the educator can seek the cause. All the major influences to which a child is prone should be investigated; home life, peer relationships, etc.

2 *Incentives.* Incentives can be very effective. A positive attitude on the part of the educator is particularly so – praise something, success somewhere, even a concrete award such as a treat. Negative incentives such as sarcasm, punishment, detention, etc. are less effective. The child may have been seeking extra attention, and such punishment may give him what he wants.

3 *Feedback.* This is a form of non-purposeful incentive. Knowing how well he can do allows a child to set his sights at an appropriate level, avoiding certain failure and easy success. Both success and failure tend to perpetuate themselves. A teacher can alter the feedback to allow a child the feeling of success and alter his outlook on learning.

4 *Group pressure.* All groups or institutions, whether family, school or ability group, exert a certain pressure on their members. If the overriding group feeling is one of rebellion, then it would take a strong member to respect established authority. Group competition can have a marked effect on group performance, but carried to extremes can be psychologically damaging. Teachers are normally supported by society in their efforts to motivate the classroom group towards learning.

5 *Transfer.* The best learning is that which can be used in other situations. The child should be able to abstract the key features from any task so that he can recognise that the same mental operations are appropriate in a superficially different task. In this way, learning is integrated with other learning at the child's own level of understanding.

6 *Action.* Learning always involves active participation, whether by sand and water play or by talking about things or by mixing chemicals. The least efficient learning process is to attend an average lecture.

Programmed learning

Teaching machines are inevitably worked by teachers and pupils and are relatively dependent on them for their effectiveness. Programmed learning, whether by book, video-tape or acoustic tape, is based on sound teaching principles and extremely high standards of lesson preparation. The learning sequence is carefully planned with regard to logical order and the need to cut boredom. The objective is to facilitate learning, children moving through the 'lessons' at their own rate. Essentially, the principle is that the learner has to make a response to a question. Having made it, he is immediately informed whether he was correct.

The use of programmed learning alone would be inflexible, but in the normal school situation, a teacher is always in charge. The essential use of feedback and the feeling of success (of some sort) which is common to this type of learning can act as a spur to individual curiosity. Programmes even have built-in encouragement and gentle chiding.

The idea of programmed learning stems from the work of Skinner and operant conditioning (see p. 32). To recapitulate: desired behaviour is rewarded by being informed you have got the right answer and by going on to the next point. In addition:

1 learning goes from simple to more complex material in an interrelated and sequential manner;
2 learning is quicker with constant and immediate reinforcement, in the form of feedback;
3 the learner may proceed at his own speed.

Technological teaching aids have not always been warmly received, but they now have their place in education. The language lab. is, at very least, a means of acquiring an accurate basis for a foreign language. It is from then on that discussion of literature and finer points of interpretation can take place.

Television as a teaching machine does not adjust its speed to each viewer. Nor does it require a response. Class instruction by television is an improvement on the single teacher only in the display of film and demonstration, which it can present in the same programme. Obviously, follow-up by the teacher is necessary to make sure that at least the majority of the children have got the point.

Teachers can implement a programme by good previous preparation and by tape-recording parts of it, to be played back at another time. If it were possible for the teacher to know programmes well, before they are relayed, it would also be possible to pre-select the viewing group so that the programme content and ability level of viewers could be better matched.

Studying

Motivation. Problems are not uncommon. Checking study aims and their relationship with motivation might reveal gaps. Mechanical action can help; directed effort is better than vague searching, just as learning in chunks is better than learning in little, unrelated bits.

(a) Organisation. Plan a rough time-table. To see that each aspect to be learned is adequately represented, let there be progress logically through the subjects, so that each follows on from the other, and is as close as possible to the outside stimulus, e.g. the lecture.

(b) Physical matters. Any noise should be quiet and constant. A heavy meal and alcohol act against learning, as do too comfortable a chair and a warm, airless room. Always having the same workplace sets the mind quickly in a working mould.

Action.

(a) Skim the work – this maps out the route to be covered.

(b) Relate new learning to old by conscious effort and questioning.

(c) Look up half-understood passages or words. Incomplete understanding helps forgetting.

(d) Summarise material, including lecture notes, in your own words. Emphasise principles in brief.

(e) Reciting aloud will quickly bring faulty learning to light.

(f) Mnemonic systems – are valuable if not too complex.

Reading. There are techniques for reading which can enhance learning: e.g. skill of scanning, avoiding vocalising, awareness of unthinking reading.

4
Social Education

The first influence on a child is the family. Each family is unique, a small mediating group placed between the greater culture and the child – so providing an individual mini-culture of its own. Child-rearing practices vary between families, even within one culture. Family make-up also varies, from isolated one-parent families in big cities to large families, integrated within a local community.

Family attitudes

The extensive long-term study headed by Douglas (1964 and 1968) has shown up the cumulative effects of family attitudes. In spite of criticism of method and interpretation, the size of the operation – 5,000 children born on one day – and the consistent re-testing has provided acceptable evidence that 'the child's capacity to do well at his work in school is to a certain degree dependent on the encouragement he gets from his parents, the sort of home he has and the academic record of his school'.

Studies of social class have shown the inhibitory effects on intellectual growth of lower occupational class. Douglas (1968) was very clear – 'The social class differences, which were considerable at the primary school stage, have increased at the secondary, and extend now to pupils of high ability.' He

39

even found an increasing difference, with increasing age, in average IQ scores between socio-economic groups. But the reports of all similar surveys reach the same basic conclusion that the biggest factor accounting for the children's variation in behaviour is attributable to parental attitudes.

The Plowden Report included a study of over 3,000 parents, which found that the number of books in a household falls with the social-class level. Several surveys argue that there is a positive relationship between family size and poor school achievement. The Newsons (1963) found that their lowest class parents were not, in themselves, deficient in language, but differed in the attitudes they held towards their children's intellectual growth. They talked fluently *about* their children, but much less *to* their children. Orders were frequent and explanation for minor queries were rare. It was communication that was faulty. Recent research indicates that children in this situation may have to develop more complicated personal strategies to extract verbal attention from their parents. Such individualised strategies would not then be likely to fit in with the school's standard middle-class procedures; thus underlining Bernstein's hypothesis (p. 24).

Jensen (1972) found that strictly economic factors, except in extreme cases, have little effect on IQ scores. He considered the culturally disadvantaged to have three main handicaps in the areas of:

1 perceptual and attentional skills
2 verbal and cognitive abilities
3 motivational factors.

(The development of perception is described on p. 17, conceptual development on p. 18, and in C2.)

Motivational factors. These are directly affected by social influences, as are personality traits; the family is strongly influential in moulding a child's outlook and psychological behaviour patterns. These behaviour patterns affect motivation, which can in turn affect future behaviour. Although there may be some basic needs, such as pain or hunger, causing changes in behaviour, they are relatively few and specific.

As a child develops, he is helped to form his own patterns of changing. Frustration of this changing, growing process can result in its time-honoured product – aggression. An example is in the crying of infants. The baby has put something into the environment – say a call for food – has received a feedback of no-food and gives vent to the ensuing anger. The resulting secondary feedback of food or no-food leads to changing expectations and behaviour. Observation by Piaget and others is that this repeated correction of expectations from perceptual impressions gradually creates the development of intellectual and emotional behaviour.

Early stimulation

The intellectual poverty of children from culturally poor homes is already noticeable by the age of five years. Perceptual deficiency is apparent in that such children recognise fewer objects and situations than middle-class children. In addition their interests are less varying, as well as being different, and they are verbally less able to describe them. Piaget (1932) pointed out three important stages in early development:

1 Firstly, the infant is essentially responsive, motivated by needs. The orienting response (seeing where you are) is present at birth, and so any changes in perceptual input will attract the infant, who will react. These reactions become coordinated until the infant begins to try and retain the stimulus change, such as the rattle waved in front of his nose.
2 Secondly, the infant shows interest and tries to keep the pleasant input going, such as being jogged on a knee.
3 Thirdly, the infant seeks novelty by a trial-and-error process, such as dropping toys from its pram and making new sounds. From the beginning 'the more a child has seen and heard, the more he wants to see and hear' (Piaget 1932). This is the beginning of intrinsic motivation, which should develop continually, given a facilitating environment.

Relatively isolated babies, such as those on large hospital wards, will obviously suffer intellectually during their first year. Babies who live in poor overcrowded conditions do usually have other children around to see to their early needs for stimulation; but when an infant in overcrowded conditions begins to move around and needs opportunities for movement and exploration, perceptual development receives a blow.

41

Later on, as a child learns to speak, he needs to be spoken to. In a family where questions are ignored or rejected and play material is strictly limited, development will become accordingly curbed. There is a possibility of sensitive learning periods but the precise effects of differing amounts of deprivation is uncertain. Maria Montessori found that children are more receptive for learning which involves colour, shape, sound and texture between $2\frac{1}{2}$ to 6 years, than at other times. If a child is taught something for which he is not ready, he may develop a dislike for it; too late, and he may have lost interest.

Achievement

The social environment affects a child's educational development continually, particularly with regard to achievement. Motivation for achievement in any direction is intertwined with the child's self-concept. This in itself is largely dependent upon the opinions of people who are important to the child. Parents' expectations and aspirations for their children can have a remarkably self-fulfilling effect. The only child, who is obliged to fulfil his parents' ambitions, does his best: the younger girl, marked down for early marriage and home-making, tends to go for just that. Larger cultural variations filter through to the family, such as the intensity of religion in that particular region, or the high regard for criminality.

Research on the 'need' for achievement, particularly by McClelland (1953), has demonstrated the effects of a type of upbringing which is relevant to educational practice. The parents emphasise early training for independence. The child is considered to develop expectations about what e.g. talking will accomplish for him, and to take pleasure from confirmation of these – as long as they have some uncertainty. Mild anxiety aids learning. In this way, the child forms a frame of reference and discovers his capabilities. If he does better than he expected, he will go on to more complicated things; if worse, his standard may drop. The crucial aspect of achievement is perceived effect in relation to self-evaluation, or in other words, positive reinforcement for proven ability.

However, parental encouragement for the child's efforts may have the opposite effect if the standards of excellence are

42

placed too high and the child fails frequently. Early attempts at mastery must be realistically matched to ability. Too much pushing towards independence may result in children merely becoming overdependent on the approval of others, such as teachers or friends. Innate differences between children in achievement motivation still remain to be investigated. A child's emotional reaction to success or failure, and indeed the scope of his frame of reference, as well as his self-confidence, may have other causes than parental approval or disapproval. These include inherited personality factors or the general social culture.

Roles

Social roles. Learning these complex roles is a part of the socialisation which all children undergo. They are similar to dramatic roles or stage parts, but are often unrecognised by the player. The development and upkeep of a role is a two-way process, especially in childhood. It involves teaching, such as 'try and behave like a lady', and the growth of the self-concept, i.e. how the little girl believes she appears to others.

The I-know-my-place attitude is still with us to some extent. Different social-class uses of language and thought have been pointed out by social researchers. Accents still separate people in Britain. Children do take upon themselves the occupational status of their parents. The son of a factory worker is more likely to find his eventual livelihood in the factory floor than a professor's son. A child's self-concept and role playing is very much tied up with that of his parents' expectations. A child, for instance, must keep to the role of a child. Should he step out of this role and make independent decisions of which his parents disapprove, this will be termed bad behaviour and due for correction. As an adult, this would be his own decision. Growing to maturity involves shaking off a number of outgrown roles; this may occur regardless of, or with the help of, influential adults.

A child's position in the family, be it first, second or fifth, can have a considerable effect on role expectations. First-born and only children strive to please their parents more, identify more strongly, and in general achieve more than their siblings.

Sex-roles. When a baby is first dressed in pink or blue, he or she has already been given a role for life. No-one would deny differences between the sexes, but of late, much that has been taken for granted about the behaviour of human males and females has become questionable.

In Western society, it is customary for boys who are going to be 'men' to learn to repress some outward show of emotion. Girls can cry, but boys are cissies if they do; girls can also seek and give affection with more approval than boys. Boys are partly expected to be tough, whereas girls are expected to be weak, both psychologically and physically.

Mussen (1965) describes how two-year-old boys and girls scream and cry equally, but by four years old, boys were hitting more frequently and screaming less frequently than girls. Erikson (1965), the Freudian analyst, observed little children at play. He found boys to be more concerned with height and downfall, strong motion (such as cars and rockets) and its swift arrest (such as by policemen). Girls were concerned with static interiors, which could be simply enclosed, and which were peaceful (like homes perhaps).

Thus in the early years, when young children are in the care of women, boys have difficulty in identifying with the adult figure and may develop a partly encouraged, self-image of naughtiness. Later, older boys have to alter this identification, which can cause problems. The influx of male teachers into the primary schools should be beneficial to both boys and girls.

Vocational choice is the end-product of this role division. Girls tend to become low-paid, low-status workers with the expectation of homemaking and motherhood as the basis of self-fulfilment. Boys are more likely to take further training and emerge with a higher-status job, expecting to work outside the home until retirement. Douglas (1968) and others have found that while parents encouraged sons to take jobs for which they were not suited in various ways, daughters were pressurised to take jobs which were generally below their ability.

As a system of prediction, one could say that the only son of a successful man was born with a silver spoon in his mouth. The tenth daughter of poor unskilled parents was unlikely to reap a rewarding life.

Personality development

Personality is concerned with individual reactions to the world. It involves abilities, emotions, perceptions and physique. For easier consideration, personality is divided into traits such as dominance, sociability, aggression, etc. (see D1 and D3).

It is not always possible or desirable to interfere with traits. The shy, introverted child may be encouraged to make friends but not forced into, for him, painful situations. The young bully's behaviour has to be seen in relation to home background. Both dominance and submission in children are closely related to the effects of strong discipline in the home.

Independence and self-confidence flourish best in a home background described above (p. 42). In addition, there should be:

1 Security and love
2 A predominance of praise for genuine effort
3 Tolerance of individual weakness
4 Encouragement in situations where help is needed
5 Some discipline, to provide guidelines for growth
6 Some teaching
7 Patience to allow a child to make mistakes
8 Situations to make a mess in
9 Facilities to try things out
10 Understanding of developmental psychology.

Children who have personality traits which make it difficult for them to mix with other children, such as fear and anxiety, may have had unfortunate life experiences. An educator needs to understand these processes to guide the child's growth. Adjustment is a continual process. All adjustment is relative; that is, there is no such thing as complete adjustment. Nor would it be desirable that children should adjust, more than is essential for living, to what can be an unhealthy environment.

Personality can be measured through behaviour, such as responses to a test situation. It has both inherited and socially induced aspects. Personality and environment react constantly, but conflict and frustration, such that a person can survive reasonably, are the source of continuing development and a creative life.

Personality and academic achievement. For some years different researchers have concluded that there is a connection between personality, as measured by the Eysenck scales of extraversion–introversion and neuroticism, and school achievement (Handley 1973, Chapter 6). Intelligence and motivation are also, of course, involved.

In brief, extraversion indicates academic success at 11 years, stable extraverts being the most likely entrants to grammar schools. During their secondary education at about thirteen years extraverted girls remain ahead of their sex, but introverted boys take the lead from their extravert peers. More recent work has shown the effect of intelligence; among those of high ability, intoverts achieved more than extraverts, but among those of low ability the reverse was true.

University entrants, then, are likely to be high ability introverts, who also have good studying ability and perseverance. What is more, they appear to get the highest degrees when measured as neurotic, in the Eysenck scale. No less than 60 per cent of stable extraverts – who have miraculously got so far – are likely to fail their finals! If the researchers could be resolutely agreed, the education services might be more economically rearranged, or at least attendance certificates could be supplied to the happy-go-lucky extraverts.

Part Two
EDUCATION IN SCHOOLS

Practical psychology in the normal school situation

5
Schools

A school is an organisation and, like other organisations, is made up of a clearly defined hierarchy of statuses. The head is at the top, and power filters down via the staff, to stop at the pupils. Sometimes pupils and other members of the school have some say in the running, but the final word is normally the head's. Very rarely, a school is run by a committee, the intention being to operate a cooperative rather than a competitive institution.

The variety of schools in Britian is immense. Two-thirds of the country's secondary schools are now officially comprehensive and are intended to bring together all the normal neighbourhood children under one roof, offering them there the widest educational opportunities that the available money can buy. In fact, they co-exist alongside grammar schools, technical schools etc., all in the same school district. It would be difficult, in fact, to point out a truly comprehensive school. Much of the ethos of any school is still due to the personality and vigour of the head teacher, no matter what the official style – and A. S. Neill's Summerhill was no exception.

The school function

The obvious purpose of a school is to educate its pupils. As part of its function, the school also attempts to implant further the values of the society which it represents and from which, on the whole, the pupils come, but schools which have a reputation for being 'good' or 'fine' are often found to select high-ability children and produce a proportionately high number of university entrants. The school which provides a stimulating intellectual atmosphere and satisfactory emotional support and guidance for children of all abilities and backgrounds may not be mentioned quite so often in the press, but can be seen to be fulfilling its functions in the behaviour of its ex-pupils.

Schools are never machines for passing out information; they always act as developmental guides, though of differing strengths. Some will leave room for pupils to grow in their own way, others act as coercing funnels, so that the emerging young person can be seen to act in the approved manner.

Schools accentuate sex-roles. Even in mixed primary schools, girls are separated out for needlework and boys learn woodwork. Secondary schools are normally divided by sex and the subject matter taught is emphasised or omitted accordingly.

In order to be a teacher who is able to apply psychology in a school, it is necessary to be aware of its functioning and aims. A teacher whose own beliefs are at variance with these, or who fails to recognise them, is unlikely to be happy there or to teach well.

Although schools largely reflect the society their pupils come from, they inevitably develop a 'personality' of their own. Moral standards tend to be higher than family morals; taking food from the kitchen is stealing, dirty clothes on children indicate moral deficiency. Politeness – 'please' and 'thank you' and opening doors for teachers – is more important than at home.

Pupil roles. Just as a child has to learn that there is one way to behave at home and another at Granny's, he must learn the pupil role. Children who go to nursery school before the age of five have learned a considerable amount about their role within a group and so 'settle down' very quickly when they get to 'proper' school. A certain amount of socialisation is essential if a child is to participate in activities with others, but the over-rigid primary school, where uniform is precise and the level of noise gives the impression of permanent examinations, also may evoke a feeling of unease for the inmates. The effects of repressive schooling can be seen in the children's creative work; attempts to fit in with the system produce stacks of dull, neatly written and correctly spelled essays, with cross-repetition of set phrases. Art work, too, tends to be stereotyped, as children learn which style gains the highest marks.

In a school where overriding importance is attached to the transfer of information, together with a noticeable imposition of discipline, good role-playing school-children will seem to be attentive and learning. But lack of real self-discipline and the stifling of intelligent curiosity in pupils is a sad educational price to pay for a smoothly running institution. This is a not uncommon feature of girls' secondary schools, particularly highly academic ones.

The high moral behaviour shown by good school role-playing is not necessarily that of a real social-moral conscience. Genuine awareness of social behaviour is a product of maturation and experience. It is an aspect of rational thinking and works independently of external social demands, as Piaget (1932) and others have shown. Such mature, rational behaviour in teenagers often appears to teachers as rebellion against the petty dictatorship of school rules, and the refusal, especially by boys, to play the obedient pupil role.

School discipline. When children begin school for the first time, they bring along a ready-made set of attitudes from home, although a very wide range of possible developments is still open. As schools are active agents of their own values and standards, difficulties can arise when home values clash with school values. Apparently minor matters, such as length of boys' hair, or girls wearing rings in school, can erupt into violent home-school altercations, showing perhaps the strengths of feelings hidden under the veneer of politeness. School uniform is often just out of fashion and teenagers can find it humiliating to be seen in it.

When the expected type of behaviour at school is very different to that of the home, children may be expected to take some time to adjust. The amount and form of control that parents have used in early upbringing, whether strict or easy-going, will notably effect the ease with which the child slips into the requirements of the school. Fortunately, when a child starts school he has the same teacher all day, so that one teacher should soon know something of him and his background. Children from homes where severe physical punishment is used are likely to be more aggressive in behaviour. Complete freedom at home also leads to a type of aggression, associated with frustration, of a child being prevented from following his own impulses in school. External control always comes before internal control and the most effective combination appears to be in a loving and supporting environment. Some internal control, the earliest form of conscience, is expected to operate at about six years old.

Many schools rank obedience and discipline as a first priority for their pupils. The child from the more authoritarian home will not find this too difficult, but the child from the democratic home may well be confused; for example, spontaneous questioning must be curbed and a certain autonomy must be forfeited. The spread of democracy from the infant school upwards is overcoming more rigid types of schooling so that even young children are becoming less bound by rules and fear of punishment and are able to construct their own education actively within the school situation.

School–home relationships

A child who spends half his waking hours in a school which all but refuses to recognise parental influence is being cheated of some educational opportunity and obliged to split his developing psychological life in two. Many a child is caught in the psychologically detrimental dichotomy of 'Miss' says this and 'Mum' says that, where Miss and Mum are never able to talk about their different opinions.

Quite apart from the financial benefits, schools which work hand in glove with parents are able to use the educational assistance which parents are mostly glad to give. A parent who can take a class round his factory, or one who describes how a car engine works, or one who listens to children reading is bringing the real world through the school gate.

Schools who deny parents as educators or who fear that, by opening the door a crack, the status of their teachers will drop, can have very little faith in their own expertise and it is likely that this attitude will be apparent in a greater rigidity and control in the school system.

A recent innovation in bridging the gap between home and school, which should work for the benefit of children and parents, is the community school. At its most open, parents and children should be able to sit in lessons together. Evening tuition and activities in the school should also be open to everyone. Although still partly experimental, this effort at educating a whole community should have a beneficial practical psychological effect on all concerned.

The school does not operate in a social vacuum, any more than the home does; both are involved in continuous interaction with the surrounding society. At the same time, they are the two most important influences on the (far from passive) child. When either of these educational influences is inadequate the child loses. Should both home and school fail to provide some aspect of educational enrichment, such as music, then apart from chance, the child may remain musically impoverished. Both home and school are, of course, equally free to supplement each other, where there seems to be a lack.

School organisation

The formal organisation of any educational institution depends upon the goals for which that institution is supposed to be aiming. The social organisation will follow from these. The spread of information and the precise power of every person in the hierarchy, unless clearly understood, can cause considerable distress, which is reflected in the teaching.

Head teachers in this country are equally free to grasp all the decision-making for themselves, or to lead a democratic school. Research on the detailed organisation of a school meets with considerable resistance, due to its 'private' nature. However, it seems, not unexpectedly, that the smooth running and contentment of a school depend largely upon how the head is *perceived* to behave by those with whom he comes in contact. An autocratic head may be seen and accepted as 'fair'; a democratic head may appear to be 'uncaring' – the greatest fault.

The social groupings of teachers in a school, whether formally or informally arranged, can have important repercussions in the classroom. The grouping of their pupils, e.g. in large or small numbers, or in ability, affects a teacher's status.

Streaming. This common type of grouping is normally made within a chronological age range, which may be coincident with a child's development age. Evidence, such as that of Douglas (1964), seems to indicate that streaming is detrimental to most children's achievement. It seems that children who are strictly streamed for lower or higher ability accept their academic positions and expect to continue to function at that level. They are reinforced in this by the effect of the streaming in that:

1 children will only come into contact with similarly selected children;
2 social experience and possibly cultural background will be limited in the form situation;
3 designated ability children will receive educational stimulus considered appropriate to their needs;
4 late developing children will fall behind in achievement which prevents catching up;
5 being labelled lower stream increases feelings of failure, and rejection, lowers morale and distorts the self-image.

The lower streams of a large school often develop clear reactions to their injured feelings in the form of poor discipline, if not real aggression. In addition, teachers in charge of lower streams tend to acquire a lower status than those with higher streams. The gap between lower-stream pupils and their teachers tends to widen, while the top streams are more able to identify with their teachers. The tenuous threads which bind education, teaching and personal relationships together are directly involved with the organisation of the school.

Ability groups. This has been called hidden streaming and must bear a warning that the division of children by ability within the educational system can have the effect of widening real or imagined differences between them. The 'Pygmalion' effect, although questioned by some researchers, is well known. In an American experiment children chosen at random were pointed out to their teachers as being highly promising. At the end of the academic year their marks were significantly higher than those of a control group of children who had not been singled out. The extent to which the teacher believes a child to be able, and the resulting expected performance, appear to be self-fulfilling.

Recent research results support the above by showing that differing amounts of intellectual stimulation with similar groups can radically alter the level of functioning of the groups. The early years of schooling in which children are normally split into groups is of prime importance in this development. Classroom organisation then, is not without its effects on individual children's scholastic performance.

Groups within the total school can be formed and reformed for various functions other than instruction. Children with special interests may be better able to progress together. Family groupings are not uncommon in primary schools, where children across a three or four year age range are grouped together for at least some parts of the day. Older ones can help the younger ones with dressing and washing and the new children are found to adjust much more quickly when they are assigned to a group of already settled children. This system can also be of advantage to a psychologically disturbed child.

Sizes of groups are not necessarily of great importance, but the purpose behind their formation will determine the value of their homogeneity, stability, freedom of expression, responsibility etc. A table of four to six children in a primary school, all working on the same subject, is not uncommon. It is becoming more frequent at secondary level, even in pre-streamed classes. More fluid grouping of children based on the learning rather than the teaching approach enables individual children to develop at their best. A clear example is in musical instrument playing, where a group of, say trumpeters, of all ages will be gathered together because of their ability and interest. This is also possible in more academic subjects where children may proceed at their own pace and style. Ability groups may be called 'sets'.

Team teaching. This is another method of crossing the one-class/one-teacher barrier, although normally children of roughly the same age are put together. Large numbers of children, even up to sixty, are taught by a coordinated group of teachers. The practical benefits to education are considered to be as follows:

1 Groups of children can be varied in size and ability to suit the task of the moment.
2 Specialist teachers can use their skills with appropriate groups.
3 Non-specialist staff and equipment can be effective, where they are needed.
4 Personality clashes between individual children and teachers are dissipated.

Harmony of purpose is essential between the team of teachers, and this feeling of cooperation should be reflected in the behaviour of the pupils. Disharmony between teachers, however, can have a devastating effect. Pupils are less likely to see their teachers in a formal role in team teaching and, when functioning well, it is a practical asset to education.

Buildings. The age and layout of a school inevitably affect the type of teaching which may take place there. Team teaching, for instance, requires space. A school built with classrooms faced with glass, round a central hall, can discourage new forms of teaching. New 'comprehensives', with miles in between each part, are believed to encourage truanting, as the pupils must travel about a great deal. The imagination of the teachers may be the prime resources for educational opportunity when buildings are old and facilities poor.

Child-centred education. In essence this is simply a term for describing how a school will attempt to provide a variety of activities, so that each child should find educational satisfaction and personal growth. There should be time for individual projects and interests to develop, so that such a type of education will not have a rigid time-table.

Child-centred education can be directed, learning being no less valuable because it is not accidental, or as a by-product of another learning situation. But any form of drilled learning would be missing; the intention being to bring meaning into learning.

Free schools. Teachers who believe that present schools do more harm than good have set up, in several cities, schools which are free from authoritarian structures and competitive atmosphere. They attract children who would otherwise be truanting from state schools. Some say this helps the state by removing its difficult cases. Radical educationalists believe that they are offering an alternative system of education to which, eventually, non-disrupters will come. So far, however, free schools can only exist in a prosperous society, where money is available from charitable grants and unpaid teachers can live on social security. The curriculum in such schools attempts to teach children what they want to learn and now official state schools for truants are beginning to work on the same lines.

6
Teachers

Motivation for teaching

Men and women, young or 'mature', stable or neurotic, can train to be teachers. They are a voluntary, self-selected population of people for whom neither ability, nor even a real wish to teach, are required qualifications. However, students cannot enter a teacher training course without having a minimum academic standard.

Applications for courses stem from a variety of motivations such as:

1 Security – a regular salary for life.
2 Long holidays – often quoted by non-teachers – which tend to get eaten away by extra-curricular activities such as courses or second jobs. Short working days come into the same category.
3 Satisfaction – the joy of teaching young minds – can, at its extreme, become the love of power over a captive audience. However, thwarted performers or autocrats are not necessarily the poorest teachers. Satisfaction also includes the constant challenge which teaching represents.
4 Respectability – however hard the work, it is a clean, reasonably high-status job, which implies superior knowledge.
5 Fits in with school holidays – a big pull for prospective or actual mothers. In this sense, it is a 'natural' choice for educated women.
6 The system promotes its own. To a person who has progressed

through school and university, with say a degree in history, or English literature, teaching may appear to be the unthinking and easiest next step.

In general, prospective teachers have themselves enjoyed being taught and are often the children of teachers. As they are unlikely to have had much experience of the outside world, the profession is sometimes said to be overly academic and inward looking, which has its effects in the classroom.

Teacher training

University graduates take a Post-Graduate Certificate of Education course, which in the space of one academic year prepares a graduate for teaching. Normally, the course consists of methods of teaching the specialist subject, theoretical educational psychology and teaching-practice under supervision. There are, in addition, various lectures, seminars and visits.

Colleges of education and education departments or polytechnics offer a three-year training for various Certificates in Education, and a further year for a Bachelor's degree in Education to students straight out of secondary school. A much wider variety of educational provision and teaching practice is possible in the longer time, which must, of course, include the subject matter to be taught. These years also form an important part of the student's own education and provide time for personal growth. Many student teachers are suffering from a degree of artistic, practical, physical or creative atrophy. This has been brought on by continual effort at passing examinations! Before students can enjoy teaching children, they should enjoy rediscovering learning pleasure and rusty abilities in themselves. But not all teacher training institutions encourage this. Mature or 'exceptional' students, admitted on prospective merit and lower exam successes, have fewer problems in this respect.

Educational psychology is an integral part of all teacher training programmes. But it is rarely presented in the form in which it may be put to immediate use in schools, being rather over-burdened with theory and academically respectable psychological topics, which are not necessarily appropriate to teacher needs. A thorough understanding of the developmental process in children is undoubtedly essential, but incomplete on its own. Psychology is also a practical tool in education, which can be used both in schools and in teacher training itself.

Field-work. Out-of-college studies are not often found in British educational psychology courses; they are commoner in other subjects, or in America. They can add valuable insight and effectiveness to the training of teachers.

1 Child study. Students may choose a child to study over a period of two years and write up a detailed case report. This includes a description of the child's home, relationships, school life etc. It is entirely confidential.
2 Shorter field-studies may involve evaluating groups of children or helping 'difficult' children, visiting and evaluating institutions etc.

Field-work has the advantage of taking students out of the academic learning situation, at least for a while, into a variety of homes or clinics, and into other people's lives. Theoretical, exam-orientated educational psychology is complementary, but not a substitute for spending time with, adapting to and learning about even one real child. Students personally involved with both normal and abnormal children will be far more aware of children as individuals.

Microteaching. This is essentially a form of short lessons in small classes, which is being used more frequently in the initial and post-experience training of teachers. A teacher prepares a ten-minute lesson for a handful of pupils and a video-tape camera records the results. The teacher watches the playback, notes his or her mistakes, and tries again with another group of pupils. The method is considerably speedier and more effective than practice with a whole class. The benefits of teacher learning through microteaching, discovered by research, are impressive:

1 The teacher's talking dropped by at least a third including:
   (a) the number of times a teacher repeated his questions, and
   (b) the number of times a teacher answered his own questions.
2 The teachers interrupted discussions less frequently.
3 The children's questions were more carefully thought out, and more complex.
4 The children appeared to talk and learn more.

60

This technique is also applicable to other types of training involving relationships, such as counselling or interviewing.

Assessment. Even with a basic understanding of development, students can have little scientific basis for judgement of the children in their care unless they are aware of the various types of assessment procedures. It is possible for teachers to become qualified without the simplest understanding of statistics, such as the possible meanings of a comparison of children's scores on an achievement test. Understanding the educational psychologist's report is not always straightforward for a teacher – though this may well be the fault of the psychologist.

Educational research. In general, appreciation of the fruits of educational research and the motivation to practice it are not given importance in teacher training courses. As a consequence, teachers place little value on research results and are often antipathetic to research work in their schools. Researchers in turn tend to avoid the type of enquiry which is disruptive to schools; thus valuable information, such as the results of different methods of teacher training, or a comparison between the benefits of different reading schemes, tend to remain neglected.

Exceptional children. Although every teacher will come across some of the problems described in Part Three, understanding and coping with exceptional children is most frequently reserved for specialist teachers. More serious problems must wait for the educational psychologist. Teachers are in the most obvious position to notice a child in difficulty and should be able, when necessary, to call on appropriate specialist help.

Counselling and guidance. A teacher's own self-understanding is a first step towards understanding others. Students who are able to make use of experimental group counselling sessions, or to practice interviewing with a video-tape camera as feedback, etc. will be more aware of themselves and others and should be better prepared for the position of developmental guide with children. Vocational guidance too does not hinge on test results, but on the understanding of individuals. Teachers are particularly responsible for the emotional development of their pupils in primary schools; it would be as well if they were prepared for this important aspect of their work.

Objectives of training. In an ideal world, teachers would still be human. The role of teacher includes that of a model for imitation, but achievement studies show that if the goal is too high and failure is inevitable, then the child gives up the struggle. Text-book-perfect teachers would never get bad-tempered, disgruntled, bored and sarcastic, etc.; real teachers do. As model adults, teachers are not, of course, wildly different from children, but they should be better equipped with maturity, experience, knowledge and self-control. However, when a student has spent some time in training and in gaining experience, some of the following attributes in his or her effectiveness as a teacher should emerge

1 Maturity and stability.
2 Knowledge of the subject matter being taught.
3 Understanding the processes of development, so that all children will be aided to learn and develop.
4 Genuine concern and respect for pupils as people.
5 Ability to fit in with the staff.
6 Awareness of the school in its social setting.
7 An open and lively mind.

The characteristics of teachers

Although teachers are as variable as any other people, the composition of the profession is partly defined by the routes taken to reach it, namely:

1 motivation (p. 58).
2 training.

The personal qualities of those who become teachers are of prime importance in carrying out the full teaching role, including its psychological aspects, and ultimately in maintaining general educational standards. Teachers, like pupils, bring their own amalgam of beliefs and experiences to school. But unlike any pupil, they are in an official position of considerable influence.

Social background. The most obvious feature of teachers is their predominantly aspiring middle-class background. The processes through which they have been sorted through the educational system, as well as via traditional attitudes towards teaching as a route to the 'white collar' life, are largely responsible. In colleges of education the women tend to come from a higher social class than the men.

Teachers, not surprisingly, tend to value the educational system which has benefited them. This attitude affects their own aspirations and their perceptions of the way in which individual pupils fit in with the system. Most teachers speak to their pupils in a form of English which is considered to be grammatically correct and suitable for imitation. Pupils whose morals, manners and out-of-school activities are patently not in the approved style, are likely to be at odds with the teacher's ideas of the 'better' ways of life. Research results indicate that teachers are more easily able to identify with and encourage pupils from higher social classes than themselves.

Personality. On the whole, teachers tend to be friendly, outgoing people, who value human relationships more than objects or the way things work. They are of well above average intelligence, but vary considerably in this. Greater differences have been found between the personalities of groups of teachers than between teachers and the general population. Primary school teachers, for instance, are happier when involved with children than sixth form teachers, who have a tendency to involve themselves with their subject and see pupils as beneficiaries.

Sex. Although most teachers, especially of younger children, are women, men are entering the profession in steadily increasing numbers. Headships of mixed-sex primary and secondary schools are also increasingly held by men. The sex of a teacher affects classroom relationships, such as identification, in both primary and secondary schools. As the head teacher's influence is so pervasive, it may be worth considering the effects of the changing balance of power between the sexes in our schools.

When a teacher succumbs to any of the various stresses which, to some extent, come with the post, pupils will suffer accordingly. No matter how adequate the social services commanded by the school, the teacher, in daily contact with pupils, must bear the major responsibility for their mental well being.

Adjustment. As schools vary considerably in their functioning, a newcomer will almost always have problems in adjusting to the type of acceptable and expected behaviour in the school. The more perceptive and flexible teacher clearly has an advantage.

Communication. No teacher can expect a perfect meeting with thirty minds, but some meetings are less perfect than others. Misperception of the self and others is a common cause of poor communication. Insecure teachers, who retreat from seeing their pupils as people, may hide behind institutional pupil-teacher roles. Teaching in role-bound perspectives can be counter-effective. An extreme example of this might be an aspirant middle-class teacher in a poor district. He might neither talk to his pupils in their own 'language', nor recognise their life-styles as being part of them – both during the school situation and when they go home again. Alienation and unhappiness are then all too probable. Communication is not only verbal. Enthusiasm, eye-contact, loving physical contact with little ones, etc. are all parts of getting the meaning across.

Authority. Not all teachers welcome their inevitable positions of authority. Refusal to accept authority in the classroom and crude attempts to identify with pupils as equals can be very confusing for pupils, who are capable of rejecting this proferred friendship quite bluntly. The blow to the teacher's self-image can be hard.

At the other extreme, true authority, which is based on respect, may be unjustifiably assumed. A teacher must be in charge of a classroom, but failure of teacher self-discipline, such as constant lateness, detectable dislike of teaching, bad teaching, shortage of knowledge, etc. will detract from authority and leave room for chaos.

Inadequate training. New teachers are now officially obliged to spend a year as probationers. But even on teaching-practice, it is not unknown for an inexperienced teacher, well tutored in the theories of teaching, to be given considerable responsibility in a very real classroom. Even with adequate training, adapting to reality requires time.

Monotony. Although it is a hazard of most occupations, teachers appear to suffer greatly from monotony. The same lessons, given to a different set of similar names and faces every year, the constant repetition of teaching points in the classroom situation, the persistent playing of the teacher role, the energy needed for constant enthusiasm. Bored teachers create bored pupils and the attendant classroom problems.

Fatigue. Good teaching requires great effort and many teachers suffer from physical and mental strain. Real emotional distress in the confines of a school can be unbearable. Other members of staff can be supportive or destructive depending on the prevailing atmosphere in the school staffroom.

Alleviations

It is probably true that most teachers are under some stress as a result of their work. Daily contact with growing, active groups of children and the sundry human relationships, implicit in an organisation of any size, demand constant energy and ingenuity. Applied psychology for teachers is not dissimilar to general prescriptions for mental health.

1 Be aware of yourself. Use someone else to help you put your actions, successes and failures, into perspective. Teachers should have the opportunity, like pupils, to have access to a trained counsellor. Group discussion between teachers is often helpful, especially out of the school setting, say at a teachers' centre. Techniques such as psycho-drama can encourage insight. Head teachers are often in lonely positions and could benefit from group meetings.
2 Respect is a two-way process. When teachers have genuine respect for all the other people in the school, as well as expecting it themselves, problems are less noticeable.
3 Rest. Teachers need real breaks during a working day. Free

time does not have to be filled by marking and lesson preparation. A teacher who finds that most evenings are spent in school work too should examine his or her methods of work and the school's expectations. Over-conscientious teachers are not always the best at making human relationships.

4 Monotony. Breaking monotony is a matter of personal judgement, which calls for constant extra effort. Changes in teaching routine, possibly putting different emphasis on the syllabus, refresher courses and an experimental, creative approach to teaching are all valuable antidotes.

5 If teaching is constantly distressful, the head seems a petty dictator, the regulations like a maze of tripwires, the school atmosphere stifling, it would seem wise to change schools. Otherwise, a long, if not permanent, break from teaching might be the answer.

7
Teaching

The crunch must come – what does one do when faced with a class of thirty or forty active young individuals? There is no short answer, no bag of tricks to reach for and no advice is foolproof. Although teaching methods and specific techniques are scattered throughout this text, more general points applicable to the practice of teaching in schools are considered here.

The teaching task

To teach involves harnessing developmental psychology so that children may make the best use of their abilities in educational terms. The teacher acts as a mediator or guide between knowledge and the child. He or she is more concerned with the processes than the product of learning for, exam results apart, the products depend almost entirely on the processes. For the pupil, it is the stability of his own personal world which is the source of his motivation, enthusiasms and feelings about life.

The teacher must be aware of educational routes, their unevenness, individuality and how to modify teaching method so as to enable pupils to prosper in spite of difficulty. For example, teaching involves encouragement when learning plateaux (see p. 35) arise and even more encouragement to keep going when learning has to start all over again.

Teaching can be a trade, a direct presentation of information from teacher – as textbook – to pupil; payment is by local authority. Developmental psychology has little place in such a situation. Good teaching is both a science, in its use of technique, and an art, evolved through the ability, experience and personality of the teacher. A good teacher is able and willing to find out and evaluate the published results of educational psychological research and possibly to incorporate some of their practical implications into teaching. But teaching is no substitute for knowledge, and paradoxically, too perfect a devotion to method overshadows the growth of good teaching.

Two basic aspects of the teaching task are implicit in method:

1 Processes – behaviour change;
2 Objectives – specified directions.

Planning. Confident, effective teaching is based on knowledge and preparation for the task. Specific lesson preparation in terms of objectives and procedures is essential, but longer term planning based on educational psychology is at least as important. Teaching always involves some incidental learning, which can be planned to a large extent. Attitude formation is a particularly important by-product of teaching any subject. The primary school child is particularly open to the teacher's own attitudes, which may be passed on unconsciously. Planning for by-products in teaching implies considerable self-awareness and knowledge of what one is doing on the part of the teacher. Long and short-term effects should always be considered in planning.

However, plans in teaching are always only possibilities or hypotheses, as no two combinations of teacher and class are ever made of the same productive mixture. Experience is valuable, but not foolproof. Plans are strategies, which are designed to bring about the desired behaviour changes. They come under test every day they are used and need constant examination of their value. The teacher is her own examiner, although external exams may appear to take over this function. If a teacher's planning is valid, i.e. accurately designed for the developmental level and abilities of the pupils, learning will proceed. If ideas misfire (a not extraordinary situation) they clearly need some revision.

Classroom climate

The atmosphere in a classroom is largely of the teacher's own making. Her attitudes to the children and the relationships which she tries to evolve with them bring about their expectations and reactions to her. There are teachers who, because of their own personality problems or immaturity, are unable to bring about a classroom atmosphere which they themselves would wish to have.

But the teacher is never entirely responsible for the situation; the general climate in the school, as well as the local variations in child upbringing, are all contributors. For example, group discussion or class laughter can raise the noise level above that thought tolerable by the school; parents who have little knowledge of modern methods complain that their children are only playing in infant schools.

The practical conclusions of the well known experiment by Lippitt and White (See B1, Chapter 6) on styles of discipline with eleven-year-old boys still waits for application in many schools. Three groups of boys were taught under three styles of harsh, democratic or uncaring leadership respectively. Only those under the democratic leadership obtained real self-discipline and gained most from their learning situation.

An authoritarian style atmosphere is certainly of value when information is to be simply handed over. Not all learning is of a discoverable nature, and even very young children can take great pleasure in memorising and learning from the teacher's directions. However, a democratic atmosphere in a classroom implies that the children will be involved in making their own learning experiences. Democratic teaching makes more demands on the teacher, who must be able and ready to pick out the children's own ideas and experiences, to help to focus partly-formed conclusion and to work with the children in building up their knowledge and autonomy. It means a certain amount of real listening and sensitive awareness. So many teachers conceive it their duty to be always teaching, when they should know through personal experience that the quickest way to learn is to teach – to explain – to talk.

A teacher's behaviour in the classroom will probably vary between these extremes during one day. The same good teacher will be able to call children to order and also to communicate real delight when Johnny grasps the concept of multiplication, while preserving an atmosphere of happy learning. A good atmosphere can accommodate many distractions, such as different teacher behaviour, interruptions, poor equipment, etc., without distortion. Over-strict or careless teaching or a constant change of teachers can disrupt harmony so that, for instance, children become unruly unless under supervision. Classroom climate is a matter of trust, learned by experience, through which children form their impressions of school and their attitudes to educations.

Organisation and discipline

The more appropriate the educational material is to the ability levels and intellectual needs of the individual pupils, the less likely are problems of discipline.

Control. No matter what the teaching method, whether drilling multiplication tables, or guiding discovery learning, the teacher should be in control of the situation. But control is relative, neither tyranny nor a free-for-all provides the optimum learning situation.

Although some schools are notorious, due to their pupils' behaviour, teachers do tend to regard difficulties in controlling a class, or even certain children, as their own faults. Discipline problems are not necessarily the results of poor teaching and class mismanagement – though this is not to deny that some are. Teachers have to work hard at getting to know their pupils, how they are developing, and what types of home conditions they live in. The rapid turnover of teachers in inner city schools works against this communication and the maintenance of a working discipline.

Social grouping. Children work at their best when they are in a friendly atmosphere with people they like. Moreno's sociometric grouping has been found to be effective. In a free situation, children choose to sit next to their friend(s). But if, instead of this, the teacher asks each child who he would like to sit next to, go on holiday with, etc., groups emerge which can be represented in a sociogram (B1, B2). Teachers can then use these groups for the most effective teaching, for identifying and maybe integrating isolates or for particular tasks which require cooperation.

Grouping children always has built-in problems, which are mostly due to their segregation (see pp. 53, 54). On this particularly fluid basis of friendship and popularity, frequent changes are advisable. Altering strategy in the classroom is in itself a stimulant, providing that it is not done to the point of confusion. Different forms of groupings are effective for different purposes and as parts of different plans. Class teaching, for instance, is a valuable forum for the primary presentation of new material, or demonstrating, putting individual ideas into perspective, integrating the products of separate group learnings, etc.

Behaviour modification

This is the current term used to describe the effects of reward (reinforcement) and punishment on behaviour. Its most recent promoter in the field of applied psychology is B.F. Skinner (1953) (see A3). Teaching machines and programmed learning are the most obvious educational applications of this research.

Learning. The constant repetition of similar conclusions, from generations of research work – that reward is more effective than punishment – is yet to be widely practised in schools.

Both praise and blame are more effective than practice alone and are at their most effective when closest in time to the pupil's behaviour. Behaviour modification is dependent on the individuals concerned. Extroverts are said to respond better to blame and introverts to praise. But the relationship between teacher and pupil is the most important. When the relationship is good, a little of either comment goes a long way; when it is poor or non-existent, punishment is particularly ineffective.

Teaching with praise calls for particular skills in the teacher, especially when children are accustomed to blame and to failure. But in praising the slightest step forward or contribution, children can be made to feel happier and learn better.

71

Praise can be given for a suggestion, a mark, an idea, a nice smile, anything. Teaching without comment, or with only a muttered 'yes', or an ambiguous tick on written work, is dull and disheartening, even to the keen pupil.

Skinner terms the processes of reinforcement in daily life 'shaping'. First a gross approximation of the desired behaviour is rewarded, then closer and closer ones. This technique is the most common form of teaching in the classroom, with or without the label. The teacher asks a series of questions to the class, beginning simply and eventually leading through logical stages, accompanied by 'good', to the solution of a problem – the teacher's problem. It is also known as the 'guess what I'm thinking' technique as there is only one 'right' solution to each question. There is no time for a pupil to think or talk around the point in question, as the teacher hurries on with his or her train of thought. Even in the whole class situation, more profit is to be gained when a teacher works with a few children, while the rest watch, than darting to different raised hands. Shaping must have feedback and, as in all learning, the learner must be alive himself.

Behaviour modification in learning is largely mechanical and has its place in schools, not least in the pleasure for the pupil from praiseful teaching, and as a basis for certain subjects in programmed learning. But as learning becomes more abstract, functioning by trial and error, conditioning and reward and punishment become less used, both for motivational reasons and because time is short.

Teaching by punishment ranges from verbal blame to physical infliction of pain and mental humiliation on children. It is known to be the least, but still effective, deterrent to unwanted behaviour. Its long-term effects upon the punished, in terms of imitation, are well known. Although some pupils are particularly troublesome (Chapter 12) and appear to conform more readily to frequent punishment, it is also worth noting that some teachers, more than others, are attracted towards this form of teaching. Their own personalities, life histories and attitudes towards their pupils will differ from those who favour other methods. Strict discipline in the classroom also has repercussions when the child goes home, depending of course, on the home situation. Stress in children is liable to erupt somewhere.

Cooperation. Behaviour modification in the western world has been concerned with the direct reinforcement of positive or 'good' behaviour of individual children in the classroom, in order to improve work output. The Russians, however, have treated that aspect as secondary and have concentrated instead on 'character development'. This is understood as a matter of developing school children's personalities so that they can work better together, improve motivation and support the communist ideology.

In a Russian experiment, many years ago, small classroom groups, in competition, were offered rewards of group status and teacher approval for 'good' behaviour. As this was done in groups, pupils were obliged to help each other in their work effort and to control each other's behaviour. The Russians found that higher work levels resulted and children developed cooperative abilities and a sense of mutual responsibility. This type of classroom organisation has become very much used there.

Recent research in an English junior school, based on the Russian model, has produced similar results. Cooperative behaviours – directing others, helping others and peer dependence – were rewarded. Each group was awarded an appropriate number of pegs and the winning group was rewarded with free time. Inappropriate behaviours – teacher dependence, aggressive behaviour, disruptive behaviour and not working – were ignored. The results of the experiment showed a distinct improvement in cooperative behaviour. There was no significant improvement in work levels in this instance, which may have been due to the particular techniques employed. But clearly, there is room for school teachers, as well as academic researchers, to actively promote research by which children's education may benefit.

Teaching for learning

Good teaching of any material also involves teaching pupils how to learn. In order to do this, a teacher must first be aware of, then able to communicate, the nature and processes of learning to the pupil. Teaching learning helps to prevent the development of faulty techniques and can set a child on an effective path for life.

Pupil goals. To get the most out of the learning situation, a pupil must know what he is aiming for and how he's doing. Young children need obvious short-term goals, which are attainable. As they get older, goals or end-products of learning can become less specific and their values can be recognised in a wider context than immediate reward. Even in sixth forms, it is not uncommon for teachers to dole out the syllabus in bits – one set book at a time – so that the pupils fail to grasp the pattern of learning which they are to pursue. It would not be an impossible burden for the teacher if the pupils were to make their own selection from the syllabus, rather than accepting the teacher's. Improved motivation improves learning.

Pupils' needs are rarely expressed in the classroom situation. Were the children to be taught to be more self-aware and able to feel free to express their needs, then guidance should be available. The teacher directs the goals, even in child-centred education, and attempts to present them to children in a variety of ways. Would it not be possible, and more educational for children of all ages, to discuss both what they are doing and what value it has with the teacher? Educational objectives, such as those of Bloom (Stones, 1970), are designed to be used by teachers, but should not be confined to them. Exercises in the setting up of objectives in learning situations are of great value to both pupils and teachers.

Young children. Teaching in tune with development is particularly important with the very young. The presentation of new information, and the methods used to convey it, form the foundation of future learning. Although most children will find most of their schoolwork intrinsically satisfying, some is less so and will require extrinsic reward from the teacher to tide over a difficult patch of boredom. Teacher approval is extrinsic satisfaction, and teachers should take care that it is spread over all the children. Often it is those who need it least who get the most praise. Recent studies have indicated that, even in primary schools, social-class differences affect a child's willingness to accept delayed satisfaction.

With increased understanding of their emotional needs, young children are now being taught by only a small number of staff so that reasonable relationships can be made between teacher and pupil. But in a situation where large numbers of immigrants are settling in the local community, their child-rearing practices may be vastly different and the children concerned may have difficulties in making relationships, both with the teacher and with the class. Even school beginners find themselves as representatives of their own culture and will be faced with relatively strange behaviours, to which they are expected to conform.

The reception class teacher is in an especially important position, as she is possibly, for many children, the first adult outside the family in a position of authority. It is her task to help the child to adjust to the needs of the group and to provide understanding of such rules as are necessary. But children under nine years old have neither the maturity nor singleness of purpose to form a true group, so that grouping should be very fluid and for specific purposes, where children are not working individually.

Effective learning, especially for young children, must be meaningful. It is best acquired through experiences that are acceptable to the child in terms of his abilities, interests and background. Teaching involves structuring the learning so that the child may partake of it, but also so that the child might create while learning. Although creativity might be thought of as an end-product of learning, it is also that continuing part of the process which enables learning to be used in all possible ways. Discovery methods of learning make hard work for the teacher. She is not a watcher on someone else's shore, but an active participant in the discovery and creation of new understanding. Perhaps it is the ability to be at once a teacher and a learner, to be as excited as the child at the rediscovery of simple learning, that requires a high degree of empathy and a true love of teaching.

Nursery teaching. The earliest education provides the first guided opportunities to explore and learn social and perceptual skills. Discoveries can be made by the child working alone, but there is always a friendly teacher to learn and talk with nearby.

A nursery teacher is particularly obligated to providing a warm, secure, maybe even peaceful, atmosphere for learning and inevitable relearning to blossom. Montessori stressed the keen observation needed by the teacher of young children so that she would be able to provide the right learning material at the right time. A sensitive teacher has respect for the smallest pupil. This means leaving a child alone when he is absorbed in an experience, refocusing attention as it begins to pall, and not assuming that all children are alike. Keen teachers sometimes assume a sort of anthropomorphic attitude towards the very young, empathising to such an extent that the teacher projects her own feelings on to the child and then reacts accordingly.

Teaching deprived beginners has sometimes been aimed at the parents. Several attempts at sending out travelling nursery school teachers into homes have met with welcome and success all round. But the programmes are still too new for full reporting.

Learning and identification with the teacher is impeded by constant 'correction' of speech and other disapproval of manners. The mere provision of attractive books and toys is insufficient stimulation for a toddler who has never learned to explore. Nursery school teachers have the means with which to broaden the level of communication and learning without conflicting with previously learned modes of intellectual behaviour (see Chapter 9).

8
Evaluation

Effort and achievement in the school should be evaluated in relation to both its functions of teaching and learning.

Evaluating teaching

To evaluate teaching is to question its effect. Far too little information is available about how much use teachers make of practical psychology, or of what they know about it. The problems of research in teaching are often due to the traditional privacy of the classroom in Britain.

The more forward-looking teacher training courses do attempt to treat students as partners in their own learning procedures. This is largely as a preliminary exercise for their future teaching attitudes, but regular self-evaluation does not come naturally to most teachers. The habit of self-evaluation and the parallel willingness to be evaluated by others imply a constantly open mind, as well as positive attitudes towards possible change in teaching behaviour.

However, research in teacher effectiveness does take place, occasionally resulting in behavioural change. Researchers are often 'planted' in a classroom to take samples of classroom interactions. Various aspects of teaching have been assessed and evaluated, for example:

Explanation. This talking activity, frequently assumed to be the most worthwhile part of the teacher's task, has been found to be surprisingly deficient 'under the microscope'. Often, vital facts or the essential explanatory principle are missing from the explanation (Morrison and McIntyre 1969, p. 151). Obviously, repetitious spelling-out of principles can be laborious and unnecessary, but teachers are not always quite clear before they start, i.e. at the planning stage, about the most appropriate and complete methods they will use to put over their points. Teachers may also make unwarranted assumptions about the general level of understanding and concept-formation of the pupils in front of them.

Sometimes, the syllabus is at fault in asking for an intellectual developmental level which pupils may not have reached, or in asking for qualities of teacher explanation which call for higher communication skills than those of which the teacher is capable. An example of such difficulty is in the two-year syllabus leading to GCE 'O' level. Pupils between 14–16 years are at very different levels of development. Depending on the group concerned, a teacher always has to decide which aspects of the syllabus to tackle before others and in what manner to present the required information and concepts.

Attention. The amount of attention a teacher gives to pupils in the class varies for reasons unconnected with teaching or learning. Even when noted unfairness has been pointed out to teachers by researchers, they are not always able to adjust their behaviour. The flexibility of approach to individual needs and the sensitivity to inexplicit cries for help from pupils may call for more teaching skills than many teachers have acquired or are willing to acquire. In the same way as with streaming or ability grouping (p. 54) teacher attention may be misperceived by, and be detrimental to, individual pupils, not only in terms of self-image but in what a pupil's classmates believe of him.

Non-verbal communication. Some interesting research findings, particularly from the study of primate societies, have thrown new light on the study of human non-verbal signalling (see B1 and B2). In ethnological terms, the teacher is by the nature of her job in a dominant position. The non-verbal cues which she transmits and is able to receive, recognise and respond to are an essential part of communication in the class-room. They might be – posture, proximity, facial expression, voice-tone, and so forth.

Work on eye-contact is particularly noteworthy. It is a more intimate form of signalling than, say, body posture. Plentiful eye-contact indicates warmth and friendliness, but dropping eyelids to focus on the desk when a pupil is present can signal dismissal or rejection.

The teacher behind her desk or 'boundary' is in her own 'territory'. She is 'safer', but shows less friendliness than one who comes out to her pupils. But too much friendliness – stepping out of role – of either pupil or teacher, can be distressing and detrimental to learning. The dual role of authority figure and friendly guide is difficult to play (p. 64).

Teacher attitudes. In Manchester, 2,000 thirteen-year-old boys and their teachers were photographed and examined over forty lessons. They were also carefully questioned. Over one million photographs, from two hundred lessons and twenty-seven schools, were examined. The results showed that, without a doubt, different and distinguishable atmospheres were present in the various schools. They stemmed largely from the attitudes held within the school hierarchy. When teachers were satisfied with the school government, their behaviour towards their pupils was significantly different to that of teachers who were dissatisfied. In turn, the attitudes of the pupils to the school were affected by their teachers' perceptions of the situation. The children's regard of the teachers, both as persons and professionals, and their affection towards them were clearly connected to the contentment of the staff. If the teachers see their superiors as remote and dictatorial, they in their turn are seen by their pupils as unfriendly and ineffective.

Teacher behaviour, as measured by tape-recorder, timed observations or film, can only be fully evaluated in conjunction with pupil development, and most teachers have many pupils. The task would be highly complex, involving many personalities and backgrounds; consequently, very little has been scientifically recorded about the real effects of teachers on the all-round development of their pupils. Nevertheless, there is sufficient evidence to believe that teachers are effective, but that they could benefit greatly from training in social skills, and also those skills more commonly associated with the use of psychology in advertising, or mass communication. Teaching is also a very old profession, which has acquired a considerable weight of unquestioned tradition. As teaching resources become more expensive, there is all the more reason for better evaluation, so as to be able to plan the most effective education for the consumer, who is also the future teacher.

Evaluating learning

Achievement testing. Although facts alone are relatively sterile, their accumulation is more readily available for assessment than any other form of learning. Research has shown that the acquisition of information does not in itself promote reasoning or transfer, although it is an essential part of those processes.

Primarily, testing achievement involves careful definition of the goals of specific teaching, and of how far the teacher expects the pupils to be along the way to their attainment. Results of testing should be used to find out how the pupil actually performs in relation to what is expected; they should also be used as tools of guidance for the teachers. The teacher will then have a valuable source of feedback as to her teaching effectiveness. The pupil should be aware of these meanings; results given as secret reports to parents do not necessarily benefit the child.

Achievement tests are beneficial to learning because:

1 They provide short-term goals.
2 They oblige the pupil to do some preparation for them, involving some learning (as well as memorising).
3 They provide learning experiences in themselves as situations of trial.
4 Good results, if returned promptly, provide reinforcement. Poor results rarely act as incentives to do better and also tend to act as reinforcers, but of poor learning attitudes.

Achievement tests are harmful when:

1 They become goals in their own right, for teacher or pupils, and dominate education in schools. They then become cur-

rency with which to buy other forms of learning and, in effect, detract from meaningful education. Some schools even have reputations as exam 'conveyor-belts'.

2 They are used as absolute segregators of children.

3 They are taken to represent a child's total development. Marks can distress children to the extent of inducing school avoidance, discouraging the child and his future progress, evoking hostility and feelings of resentment, unfairness, etc. Low designation can also interfere with good teacher/pupil relationships.

4 They interfere with other aspects of development.

5 They are virtually the only indications of a child's progress, which a school communicates to parents. The parent may not interpret the same meaning as the teacher intended.

6 They are accepted as valid and worthwhile, when in fact they may be giving a completely false picture of academic achievement. This may be for reasons of poor testing techniques, or poor marking and comparison techniques. Maybe it is a matter of dislike between pupil and teacher, or a favouring of certain pupils by teachers. In some schools, some pupils cheat with the knowledge of the teachers, and the more honest pupils are then penalised.

Devising tests. More precise statistical details are to be found in recommended textbooks and especially A8 of this series. Just a few essential points are mentioned here.

(a) Validity. The test procedure should measure what it is intended to measure. Do the questions really search for answers in the named subject under test, or is general knowledge, for instance, a large factor in the expected replies? Is the marking affected by other 'subjects', such as the lowering of geography marks by bad spelling?

(b) Reliability. The test should produce much the same result if given again to the same pupil within a short space of time – it should be consistent. Every individual will vary at different times, leaving some room for error, but there are limits to the acceptability of this error. A test can be totally reliable and yet not measure what it is intended to, i.e. not be valid. But a test which is valid is always reliable.

Tests which require short cut-and-dried answers, i.e. objective tests, are easier to mark and more reliable. Essay-type answers are found to receive marks which vary from teachers of the same subject, even when marked on specified points;

impression marking is very little inferior and much quicker. But it is in the essay-type answer that reasoning and selection are best measured.

Teacher-made tests – either end-of-year exams or spot tests during the term – should be equally valid and reliable feedback tools. This may be helped by:

1 being able to use appropriate and varying measuring methods;
2 being aware of the means by which a test can be formed, so that most pupils will score around the 50 per cent mark, or wherever the teacher wants them to score;
3 making questions clear and specific, particularly for essay type answers.
4 making different questions, if these are options of as equal value as possible;
5 building up a continual stockpile of questions;
6 being aware of simple statistical procedures such as the standardisation of scores and the difficulties in comparing the results of different tests.

Non-testing assessment. Continuous assessment is becoming more popular, but has its limitations. Essentially, the teacher keeps a record in marks or words of how each pupil progresses. This may be a totalling of essay grades, or a note of the quality of cakes baked. It is not as decisive as an examination and has all the bias of being marked by one examiner, who is also the teacher, but is possibly a fairer overall estimate of the pupil's abilities.

Open-book exams are another technique devised to avoid the apparent examination of rote memory in a formal exam. The examinee is allowed to bring any information into the exam. This avoids rote memorisation of mathematical or chemical formulae, for instance, or information which a professional would look up rather than remember. Pre-knowledge of examination questions could come into the same category.

Dissertations or presentations of original work are taking some or all of the role of examinations. They have the benefit of avoiding exam 'nerves' and also testing the ability of the examinee to ask questions.

Self-evaluation is perhaps the least used and yet important aspect of education. Pupils who are partners in their own learning – helping to set up objectives, devising routes by which to reach them, etc. – will obtain the greatest benefit from self-evaluation and testing, which they have been involved in preparing. It is their very own feedback. If the pupil accepts self and school evaluation as an integral part of his education and is not restricted to judgement by the system alone, then he will be aware of what he is doing – and for what goals he is aiming. Self-evaluation also provides the pupil with an important lesson in self-understanding – a most vital aspect of education. But the validity of self-evaluation is uncertain. Some personalities tend to over- or under-estimate themselves. Pupils will need help in this too, both in insight and self-acceptance.

Psychological effects on assessment. The same form of assessment, given at the same time to a number of individuals, will possibly be distorted for a number of reasons:

1 The pupil may misinterpret the test instructions. Such mistakes are not necessarily due to common-sense reasons, but to unconscious motivation, such as failure as a form of rebellion against authority.
2 Some pupils are better at getting down what they know than others, possibly due to attitudes towards tests, feelings of security, and general intelligence.
3 Some pupils are better at recognition than recall; test results will then vary with the form of the test and the dominant preceptual modes of the pupils.
4 Health, both physical and psychological, is very important in intellectual functioning. Marks for instance for pre-menstrual girls are found to drop significantly, as also do those of hay-fever sufferers in July, etc.
5 Motivation is vital to the production of the best efforts the pupil can offer. Poor motivation has a variety of psychological causes.
6 External conditions, such as noise or heat, will affect some pupils intellectually more than others.
7 Interaction between tester and pupil is known to affect results. In America, for instance, black pupils have been found to score more highly on intelligence tests with black testers than with white testers.
8 Pupils are subject, like anyone else, to fluctuations in memory, attention, blockage of knowledge – often affected by differing levels of anxiety brought about by the examination situation and all the above conditions.

Assessing non-achievement

The assessment of the mental faculties which schools are expected to promote, other than information processing, is very difficult for a non-specialist. There are various tests on the commercial market which are available to people with appropriate experience and qualifications. Teachers can use some; others are restricted to psychologists. The National Foundation for Educational Research, Test Division, 2 Jennings Buildings, Windsor, Berks. SL4 1QS, will provide information.

The types of tests referred to are those of reasoning, of different kinds; of productive thinking; of social adjustment; of creativity, and many more. None of these tests, although often nicely packaged and presented with a backing of years of research, is an absolute measure. No one figure can ever convey all of whatever aspect of a human being is being measured. Some tests give their results in 'profiles' of, say ten figures, along a spectrum of possibilities; others in terms of percentages. All the tests which are available to teachers ask 'what' is happening rather than 'why'. Tests also measure present performance, rather than future potential, which has to be guessed. All test results should be accepted for what they are – a comparison with others on that particular test. Reading other information into a test or 'improving' the test in any way renders it invalid, that is, it alters what the test measures. More on non-achievement assessment will be found in Chapter 10 of this book and D4 and E2.

School reports

The use of forms which teachers fill in, two or three times a year, to report on pupils' progress has been much under attack of late. This is for the following reasons:

1 If marks are not standardised
     (a) marks or grades, given in different subjects, are mostly not directly comparable. Miss A is a 'stricter' marker than Miss B;
     (b) ranking in order of marks is meaningless. If several children tie and marks are similar, then a position of tenth may be virtually equivalent to first.

2 Grades often cover a multitude of ignorances on the teacher's part. She has perhaps over a hundred to fill in, within two days, but parents expect them to be accurate.
3 They act against teacher/pupil cooperation.
4 Parents tend to become emotional about reports. Seeing something in writing, from 'authority', about one's child can affect the calmest parent. Children are, on the whole, their parents' representatives.
5 Teachers may not have meant to say what parents have understood. What does 'fairly good' mean, for instance?
6 It is an extremely time-consuming and irritating ritual for the teacher to complete, and teachers tend to copy each other in their comments. Hence, good reports become better, and poor ones worse.

Adequate, freely flowing home and school communication can dispense with reports. A brief phrase on each topic can never be enough to provide understanding, and misunderstanding can wreak havoc. Pupils can indeed report on their own progress, given the respect and knowledge of having a place in the active educational team. Such pupil reporting implies trust all round, between pupil, school and home. But it might not be a bad thing to aim for.

9
Counselling

With the best will in the world, there are unlikely ever to be enough resources in schools to provide for the full needs of every pupil. To make the best possible choices, therefore, from what is available – in terms of both education and pupils' abilities and personality – some skilled help is required.

Primary schools

Self-discovery. Every child is actually potentially his own psychologist. His ideas of himself and others have accumulated from birth and are woven into the pattern of his own life, to become the experiences by which he judges himself and others. Although counsellors, as such, for nursery or primary schools are not even a twinkle in an administrator's eye, the training of teachers at that level is of vital importance in the formation of children's self-concepts and views of the world.

Training of primary teachers always includes educational psychology, but is somewhat deficient in the training of teachers as counsellors. After all, there are theoretically so many in the team – remedial teachers, welfare workers, psychologists, etc. – that there seems little need. But the teacher does have the most profound and regular influence on the child's expanding world. To teach understanding of the self and others to a little child provides an outlook and a basis for life relationships.

When asked to list their qualities, little children use terms of praise and blame with regard to:

1 social criteria
2 their relationship with their parents
3 some self-developed attitudes, depending on age.

The self, as seen by a young child, is largely determined by others. Acceptance or rejection of the image a child forms may be the result of misperception. No age is too young to begin self-discovery.

To teach psychology to primary school children is not to teach academically, but to allow a child to be consciously aware of thinking and feeling in the situation in which it happens. Plenty of potential opportunities already exist in, e.g. group projects or physical education. Group discussion and evaluation after an exercise is not beyond five-year-olds. Nor is there any reason why little ones should not be taken into the confidence of their teachers about their learning programme. It's not so much a case of 'learn this because it's best for you', but 'what do you think about numbers?' The interaction between seemingly rational intellectual processes and emotional growth forms part of the growth of the self-image and any gap is detrimental to development.

The term 'counselling' implies some form of trained intervention, but what else is teaching, in its fullest sense? Learning about life is a primary part of primary school life; learning about relationshps and how to learn should be as much a planned part of the curriculum as numbers and letters.

Confidence and learning. It has been found that by fostering a child's social and emotional abilities, the rate of learning of almost anything improves. Concentrated subject learning is possibly less effective. A recent book by Dennis Lawrence (1973) describes his research, which demonstrated that 'the child's emotional life is the most crucial factor in reading'; in this, the self-image is particularly important. He noted that reading problems and emotional disturbance were linked, but that only the reading aspect had been investigated. He divided children with reading problems into four groups of twelve each:

group 1 – received remedial reading only

87

group 2 – received remedial reading and counselling
group 3 – received counselling only from the psychologist
group 4 – received no special treatment.

'At the end of a six-month period, the children in the coun-
selled group [2] showed a significant rise in reading attainment over all the other groups, together with improved self-
images as measured on the Children's Personality Question-
naire.'

Counselling, in whatever guise, is not a panacea for all academic ills. The teacher is not a qualified psychologist, nor a
counsellor, and yet she must learn to employ their methods
within her scope. Promoting confidence is perhaps the prime
function of this aspect of the teacher's task. Children with
learning 'blocks' have already quite accepted that they cannot
cope. When a child has developed such attitudes, the teacher
has various psychological techniques available, which can help
her prepare an effective learning programme to get a child out
of the trap. For instance, young children respond well to dis-
guised, tension-free learning, in the form of games or a temporary lowering of standards to allow success to breed more
success.

Communication. Talking and listening to young children is a
technique of teaching/counselling which is often lost in the
daily business of washing and dinner, etc. Children sometimes
need to learn to speak in the bustle of the school situation. The
most helpful activity of the teacher is to listen and in doing so,
to be aware of the purposes of the child's attempted communication. Although children do learn from each other, they learn
considerably more with the well-prepared and sympathetic
teacher, who encourage talking and listening.

It is sometimes said that he who talks most learns most –
which reads like a recipe for chaos in class, but in fact, not all
the children want to talk at the same time. Thinking and language go together; teaching one's peers can be very confidence-
building, especially when writing progress is slower than the
thinking and imaginative abilities of a child. Talking always
has content, which in turn draws upon knowledge and strategies of explanation. Talking about an event often helps to put
it into perspective and to give the event meaning. It is a type
of reinforcement of the experience. Communication is in itself

a skill, which should be a part of the activities of both teachers and taught, especially with regard to young children (see A6 and Tough (1973)).

It was pointed out in Chapters 4 and 5 that children first come to school with attitudes ready for the experience. The lengthy work of Hess and Shipman (1971) has indicated the differing 'styles or strategies that the young child develops in interaction with his mother' and brings on to school. They conclude that the learning ability of the culturally disadvantaged child will become permanently limited unless there is a positive teaching effort which seeks to re-educate the child's learning abilities into more effective manoeuvrings. Positive intervention would seem inevitably to take the counselling approach, rather than straightforward passing on of information. The first move is essentially one of starting to bridge the cultural communication gap.

Secondary schools

The school counsellor

With older age-groups, teachers become specialists and are consequently less concerned with their pupils as people and more with their proficiency in the subject taught. This is probably sufficient contact for some of the pupils, but many need considerably more personal help. Teachers, for reasons outlined in Chapter 6, are not always the best people to provide it. However, there is some confusion over what a purpose-appointed school counsellor is supposed to do. In practice, this varies between the schools where these unusual people work. The concept of school counselling implies that one person in proportion to several hundred schoolchildren shall be available to help to enable pupils to grow emotionally, and to arrange the best possible educational provision within the given limits.

A number of counselling/consultations centres for young people have recently been opened in urban areas in different parts of the country. They were promptly swamped by requests for help on all sorts of personal problems and the waiting lists for attention are growing. Pupils are staying on longer at school, but this does not imply that they are better able to cope with their problems. In fact a 'difficult' schoolgirl is possibly less easy for parents to respond to than a girl who has just left school and started work. Teenagers seem particularly glad to have someone to turn to who is not a member of the family.

This chapter is concerned with counselling in the therapeutic/helping sense, the aim of which is a pupil's self-awareness and direction of his own behaviour. It is mostly, but not necessarily, non-directive in nature; that is, it does not praise, blame, or offer advice, but merely accepts what the client says about himself. Vocational guidance, which is more directive, follows in Chapter 10. School counselling is never restricted to the person appointed for the job; warm-hearted teachers will continue to be involved with their pupils when they are needed. Were teachers to be given the time and training, it is reasonable to suppose that there would be no need for the official school counsellor as such. However, no-one has yet asked the pupils where they would prefer their counselling to come from.

Counsellor and teacher behaviour. Sometimes, official school counsellors are also part-time teachers. The two behaviours are largely incompatible and can involve the hybrid person in dramatic role changes. These are mostly concerned with authority and direction – as teacher; and listening and gentle guiding – as counsellor. All forms of communication, including non-verbal, go into even temporary relationships. For example, what is the immediate reaction of pupil and teacher/counsellor on meeting in the corridor?

Teachers have their place in the school as institution; counsellors, on the whole, have not. Teachers have a job to do and must be seen to be doing it; the counsellor is private and exempt. My own research has shown up some discord between certain types of teachers and their idea of someone employed 'merely' to listen to pupils' problems.

As yet, the school counsellor is the only representative of the helping professions actually based in schools. Where the counsellor is truly a working part of a close-knit team of say, school social worker, educational psychologist and psychiatrist, then future possibilities emerge. Perhaps pupils could be helped through a phased-out school-leaving process – learning while earning – or the school counsellor could help out in the first year at work, etc. The training of counsellors is interdisciplinary. It is wasteful of resources to use them in specific office-based, school situations.

The counselling task

Counselling is an attempt to help the pupil towards understanding, and being 'at home' with himself – also called self-actualisation or autonomy. The aim is to facilitate a fully functioning person, who is sufficiently well adjusted to his life circumstances to cope with them. It is a form of mental hygiene.

As with teaching, there are a variety of theories of counselling. Practitioners are either drawn towards those they feel happiest with or take from each what they want and feel is useful at that time, i.e. they take an eclectic approach. Counsellors, too, are human and hold attitudes.

The counselling interview. The psychologically important points in a two-person situation are probably best outlined in this summary of Carl Rogers' (1965) views on the successful interview:

1 Both client [pupil] and therapist [counsellor] are affected by each other.
2 The client is in a vulnerable and anxious state.
3 The counsellor is not anxious.
4 The counsellor unconditionally accepts, and has a good regard for the client.
5 The counsellor experiences real understanding of the client's personal world.
6 The client is aware of all this.

In addition, some particular points which should or could be part of the counselling interview follow:

1 The initial impression is one of a friendly and entirely permissive situation.
2 The counsellor's language is comprehensible and leaves room for all types of response, such as 'I see' or an encouraging 'um'.
3 Silence is to be expected and used with patience. It can be broken with, for example 'Tell me more'.
4 There must be control – some direction of ebb and flow of conversation, and of bringing the interview to an end.
5 There must be non-verbal communication – words are often

91

not as meaningful as actions with adolescents. Shyness and constant headaches, as well as body expression, can be examples of non-verbal communication.

6 Recurring ideas or statements by clients are clues to deeper feelings.
7 Measuring instruments are not often called for.
8 Clients may react strongly to counsellors – and use them to 'work out' their aggression.
9 The counsellor gets the client to see his own strong points – but the client comes to them himself.
10 The counsellor gets through to the client the idea that time is needed to solve problems, i.e. one session is unlikely to right the world.

Group counselling. Most of the above points hold good in the group situation. But there are additional points with groups, for instance:

1 They can be already in existence, e.g. they may be a class in a schoolroom, or a special therapy group.
2 The participants are not necessarily in any form of distress.
3 More relationships are involved, but the group functions as a whole, a set of relationships, from which group needs, group identification, and so on, evolve.
4 People in groups also counsel and receive counselling from each other.
5 Various psychological reactions, such as identification or rivalry, are evoked in different members to the same group event.
6 Joining a group evokes feeling of similarity with other group situations, like e.g. school.
7 Controlling a group situation calls for different skills in the counsellor from controlling a one-to-one situation.

There are many theories and methods of group counselling; the various types of encounter group, the T-group, the sensitivity group, psychodrama etc. Each type of group activity attempts to help the individuals involved to become more aware of themselves in relationship to other people. The depth of emotional involvement varies considerably from the relatively formal T-group, which is used in management training, to the all-night marathon encounter group which can have violent effects on a person's self-concept.

The methods may differ but the aims are the same – to allow each member to function fully (see B2).

92

Reporting. A counselling situation is most often based on the assumption that the client wants help, varying from simple information to psychotherapy. It may involve three functions for the client:

1 Learning; improved functioning
2 Personality development
3 Self-knowledge – better perception of the client's behaviour and how it affects others.

Part of the counsellor's expertise is in recording what has happened, since

1 sheer memory is probably faulty, due to recorder bias, etc.;
2 verbatim notes miss about 50 per cent;
3 a tape-recorder is the most thorough, but requires permission from the client, and is very time-consuming in replay;
4 a pre-rated or coded form is a good compromise, but can restrict the recording breadth. Perhaps several types of form could be used.

Validity is important in both counselling and reporting. It is not unknown for clients to 'take in' gullible counsellors. Facts and other's points of view may have to be checked. This may call for particular tact and ability to withhold pupils' confidences in the school situation.

Counsellor selection

In Britain, teachers are selected for counsellor training courses, mostly because they apply and have adequate qualifications. Not all who succeed in being selected are suitable for their future role. Extra training is one method open to teachers of increasing their salary. Future school counsellors need to be particularly stable and intelligent people, with plenty of experience of school life. Their role is to be pillars of strength as their clients, and perhaps they themselves, undergo psychological change. School counsellors who are perhaps less happy in the therapeutic role can seek refuge in administration and testing. That is, of course, if they are given the choice.

10
Educational Guidance

Both educational choice in school and preparation for training and work among school-leavers are extremely haphazard in Britain at present. It seems reasonable to suggest that the majority of young people do not even make the best choices for themselves, since they have little if any personal guidance. At its best, such advice would take into consideration:

1 the pupil's abilities
2 the full range of opportunities available
3 the pupil's personality.

Careers teachers in schools and Youth Employment Offices are not sufficiently equipped to meet the needs of every child. Parents and teachers of varying ability in fact take on a good deal of the guidance task. Unit E of this series deals with vocational matters outside school. This chapter is concerned with the child who is still at school; although the influences of society outside are included.

Educational choice

Educational awareness probably begins with school. Young children, in their experimenting, become aware that they are better at some things than others and better than some children at some things. But also, from time to time, they discover

94

new abilities and new attractions. As they grow older and move into a higher school, 'authority' (in the form of subject teachers, head teachers and local education authorities) will make educational decisions for them, such as in school selection, or ability selection within the school. It is in the secondary school that the fruits of what has been (at very least accidentally) a type of educational direction or guidance really begin to define what a child will learn.

Purposeful and continuous educational guidance has been found, in America, to improve achievement, to increase students' chances in higher educations and work and to reduce delinquency. Such guidance must bring about self-awareness and some ability at self-direction. This is both the most difficult to grasp and yet the most valid form of guidance. It is here that counselling, as described in the last chapter, has its role in educational guidance. A sense of identity in a pupil implies the ability to ask, if not answer, the following questions:

Who am I?
Where do I want to go?
How can I get there?

But the wise guide and the wise child know that development involves change, and that final decisions made in early adolescence may be regretted later. It is not untrue to say that the work choice of the next generation rests on fourteen-year-old shoulders. Choosing GCE 'O' level and CSE exams by individuals has inevitable repercussions for the nation. These decisions are not immune to 'fashion', or what appears to be sensible at the time in terms of future goals. The longer educational choice can be left, the better. But delay works against the interests of a school's examination record, especially at GCE 'A' level, and so pressure to choose is inevitable at present.

The practice of educational guidance

Choices between educational options made during the school years are a preliminary to the essential vocational and higher educational choices which the school-leaver must make. The processes of selection within the school curriculum may stimulate vocational thinking, but restrict future choice.

The careers teacher. This job may be taken by the school counsellor, an untrained teacher, whoever happens to be around at the time, or may be simply ignored by the school (especially girls' schools). Their function is to enable the child to acquaint himself with a realistic picture of his abilities; it is not to coerce a child into a convenient 'slot', which a school or employer happens to have available. To 'advise' on careers is mostly a counselling type activity; group counselling is also useful for educational guidance. The counsellor must have considerable sensitivity to the vast variety of educational possibilities and moves that a pupil might make. For example, strong motivation or parental expectation is able to take a child into unpredictable realms of success. Children of mediocre academic ability can jump unexpected exam hurdles, or search out for themselves unconventional routes to attain their goals. Some children react equally strongly to expressed teacher doubt with an 'I'll show 'em' super-effort.

The youth employment officer is a useful ally. His department takes parties of children round work establishments, gives lectures and does its undermanned best to display the real world of work to school children.

When a school has a qualified careers teacher or educational counsellor, he will be able to use ability or aptitude tests as tools of guidance. Record cards of children's progress through school are as open to distortion as school reports and should be viewed, if at all, with equal suspicion as bases for decision-making. All coursellors should attempt to accept their clients as they are and not assume opinions from other people who have been involved with the child.

Educational guidance tests. Points to bear in mind:

1 There are other methods of assessing ability.
2 Tests never replace counselling.
3 Tests may not be valid, i.e. not measure what the tester wants them to.
4 Tests may detract from other aspects of guidance.

Various types of tests are available (see p. 84) which must be used both in the knowledge of how they are composed and of where they fit in to the guidance concept. They can be used in selection, from the school's point of view, or for guidance in helping an individual reach for educational decision. There are tests of:

1 general mental ability – These result mostly in an IQ score and are mostly only available to educational psychologists, although some general ability tests are available to teachers;
2 attainment – These measure progress made and not potential; they can be used to diagnose success or failure, as compared with other children;
3 aptitude – again, it is performance that is being tested; aptitude is a qualified guess, based on performance. Such tests include manual dexterity, reaction time, music, space orientation, etc.

Tests have their place in the educational guidance interview assuming that the user can confidently answer the questions:

What test shall I use?
What does it involve?
What do I do with the result?

Deficits of testing. Testing for curiosity or for filling up record cards is probably valueless. Testing without proper objectives is equally so, for example – 'What is a good test of English for eleven-year-olds?' Tests may be used as crutches or as an escape from the real problems which only patient counselling can help. They may also be used to give the tester a feeling of power, and to impress the other members of staff!

Benefits of testing. Sometimes the pupil really wants to be tested and there may be no reason why he shouldn't be. Using the results of the testing as a stimulus, both counsellor and pupil can work on from there. It is possible that tests can uncover unknown areas of ability, so that all the pupil's educational options will be on view – like on a supermarket shelf. Used in this way, tests can improve a child's self-concept and self-guidance. Testing can be used as a learning process in decision-making; pupils can choose their own tests, where there exists time for both preliminary explanation and discussion and an educational atmosphere of pupil participation.

Response sets. This is a form of perceptual set (p. 17) which distorts the interpretation and responses to tests. It may take one or more of the following forms:

1 acquiescence – pupils agree with all questions. A possible sign of immaturity;
2 evasiveness – some questions may be missed, which may be due to personal problems, lack of motivation, or extreme cautiousness;
3 extremes responses – are possibly due to relative instability;
4 social desirability – responding in a manner which the pupil believes correct; a common fault in 'nicely' brought up children;
5 speed – some tests are timed, and slow, careful pupils will be penalised.

Classification schemes

Each person who attempts educational guidance will probably devise a scheme or checklist of his own. A comprehensive interest list, to be filled in by the pupil before interview, is helpful. But various inclusive schemes, designed for use with earlier age-groups; see Hopson and Hayes (1968). The schemes presented – such as Alec Rogers' 'Seven Point Plan' for clients, or McKenzie's classification 'dimensions' of occupations – attempt to provide a sound, broad-spread system for coping with the multitude of vocational problems.

It is impossible, within these schemes, to allow for the quirks of human nature. Accidents of birth order, personality effects on achievement, personal problems, etc. must be given due weight by the sensitive counsellor.

Some influences on educational directions

The same influences which are responsible for a child's educational performance will largely contribute to its future direction.

The ethos of the school. Most grammar schools assume their pupils will go to university, and play down their practical subjects in favour of the academic. Schools in culturally poor areas tend to be less ambitious for their pupils. Teachers' attitudes and expectations are important too.

Roles (see p. 43)

1 Social-class roles can encourage or inhibit a child from doing well at school. A boy who 'knows' he's destined for the factory floor and a good starting wage is less likely to put considerable effort into his school subjects.
2 Sex roles are well documented as to their inhibitory effects on girls' ambitions and the opportunities available for their higher education. This shows itself in the minute proportion of girls released from work to colleges of further education or encouraged to go to university (as distinct from teaching or nursing) or to any of the posts of higher responsibility in business. Girls are normally given career advice (if at all) with reference to a future necessity of working part-time or of stopping work for life in their early twenties. The stereotyped role of wife and mother is quite out of step with much female behaviour today.

The adolescent sub-culture. Although there is some variation around the country, adolescent attitudes towards 'the system' are fairly uniform. The call for pupil representatives on committees which run schools and on the local education authority, the demand to be included in decision-making of curricula, the right to be heard and to have that hearing acted on, is being felt by teachers. Pupils are putting in less applications than ever for university places, especially in the pure sciences – though the social science faculties are packed to capacity. This may be said to show a heightened social awareness. Truanting or dropping-out and violence are supposedly more common; conformity, especially to authority, is out.

Group pressure from peers can be powerful in changing an individual's life course. A counsellor would have to be very isolated to avoid being acquainted with some of the most pervasive influences.

Maturation (see Chapter 2). As children develop and mature at different rates and styles, good guidance over time is essential. Of course, it is difficult to predict a late-starter, even with experience. But general physical maturation is often a guide to emotional and intellectual growth. Late maturation may prevent a child joining the 'A' stream, or bring about some psychological disturbance. The early maturing fourteen-year-old boy may develop an intense dislike of school and simply mark time until he is free to pursue his own way of life. Stress in adolescence is often due to maturational causes and the difficulty of accepting an ever-changing self-concept. Unfortunately, important educational choices are normally made at such a time.

The media. Many more opportunities are now available to school leavers in new fields. Daily contact with the media in the form of television, radio and newspapers frequently provides incentives to join this apparently glamorous band of communicators. Ways and means are set out in *The Other Careers* by Bygrave, Goodman and Fordam (1973). It is hard for careers teachers to keep themselves aware of the constant changes of opportunity for their pupils.

Vocational choice

All that has gone before contributes to the eventual career decisions (see E3). But even when decisions have been made, they are not infrequently remade. University courses are changed, or whole ways of life are altered. That in itself is not a bad thing and can bring on a new lease of life. But how often could all that disruption and heartache have been avoided by proper, professional guidance in the first place.

Part Three
EXCEPTIONAL
CHILDREN

Exceptions and psychological problems in children in
the normal school

The preliminary processes of normal educational development
are summarised in Part One. Only the exceptions to normal
development are considered here in Part Three. It is strongly
recommended that Part One be re-read at this point.

11
Slow Learners

Children who have difficulty in learning pose great problems both at home and in the classroom. From the child's point of view, the learning situation can become very depressing, if not intolerable. Then, maybe he makes some advance and life looks rosier again. The teacher has good reason to be confused with these extreme changes of mood and behaviour. How is it that he can learn sometimes, and be a complete blank at others? The answer lies in the nature of the learning problem, in where the disability shows itself and in how the individual child reacts to it.

The observer is like a super-detective; she has lots of clues, but not only does she have to pin down the causes of the learning disruption, she must also try to alleviate them. Ordinary parents and teachers are often able to understand the problems and be of help, but they are limited. It may be necessary to call in someone else – an educational psychologist or a specially qualified teacher – to add his extra training and experience to the problem situation. Slow learning is due to many causes, which are rarely found singly but tend to come in clusters (see F2).

Abilities

It may seem an obvious point that children without the appropriate ability cannot learn the task. But this is only one of many possibilities to be considered with a slow learning child. It is not unknown for a child to be labelled 'stupid' or 'clumsy', when, for instance, some form of poor but improvable hand-eye co-ordination is responsible. Spastics were accepted as being of very low intelligence until fairly recently. We now recognise the condition as one of brain-damage, affecting muscular control. It merely gives the impression of abnormal intellectual functioning.

Some children's rate of intellectual development is very slow and even though it may take the normal pattern it will still be limited in its upper level. Such children will clearly not benefit from the normal classroom situation. But unfortunately, unless they are obviously severely handicapped in intelligence, it is quite likely that they will remain in a normal school for a minimum of two years, until they transfer to a special school on the recommendation of an educational psychologist.

If dull children are left to fend for themselves, without a special curriculum, they will be obliged to wait uncomprehendingly and without learning for many hours each day, while the rest of the class 'gets on'. They can be docile watchers, but they can also be a considerable source of disruption in the class. Aggression or, at the very least, activity to break the tedium, is a well known outcome of frustration. The same condition of non-comprehension will apply to other children, who *have* the required abilities, but who for various reasons, as described in this chapter, might reasonably be called slow learners and in need of special attention. Without this special attention, children with neurological or developmental faults will certainly suffer in their eventual intellectual growth.

Developmental disabilities

Sequential development. Meaningful learning is related to previous learning and activities. If a child's developmental growth misses a sequence, it is probable that he can then only acquire a form of unrelated, non-meaningful learning.

A classroom of thirty to forty primary school children is a not infrequent source of isolated bits of learning. For instance, a child is quite happy to sound the word 'cat' when presented with a card on which there is a picture of a cat, and CAT written above it. The child may not have the faintest idea about those marks above the picture, but teacher is pleased, so he must have done well!

Making the child's hand move to form those letters comes into the same category. A teacher can make a child grasp a pencil and draw lines, which to her form letters and to him are as meaningless a piece of learning as any other form of conditional response. During what should have been the stage of learning to co-ordinate physical movement and sight, there has been a gap. Communication between hand and eye, a sequence of normal developmental learning, is missing.

Sensory development. As normal infants learn to differentiate perceptions, they come to select and control their own reactions to them. Depending on their early stimulation, children build up a repertoire of perceptual skills, of varying degrees but of a sufficient level for the normal classroom. Where stimulation, such as speech, has been severely deficient, the child is limited in his auditory skills and can only make clumsy perceptual choice, i.e. he will probably have communication problems. Reading, too, depends upon the ability to make fine discriminations between written or printed letters; d and b, for instance, are frequent problems.

Co-ordinating perception. As sensory discrimination becomes more precise, so accordingly should the response to it. In this way, far and near receptor information should come to be co-ordinated and the infant becomes more able to cope with its life. Until and unless this happens, behaviour bears little or no relation to information.

Motor information comes from physical movement and has a clear feedback; visual and auditory information does not. When a child cannot co-ordinate, he is able to 'read' and yet not understand, to receive instructions and yet not be able to carry them out. Teachers repeat the spoken instructions without effect. What is needed is a form of bridging communication so that both motor and sensory information is on the same wavelength, and can be reinforced as such. Co-ordination is a very complicated neural process and takes many years to be completed in a normal child.

Sensory perception must be matched to motor action, not the other way round: 'It is important that the match be made in the proper direction' (Kephart, 1971). In other words, sequential development must be kept in the natural order. Motor information is also the more reliable. When children get matching the wrong way round, perceptual response is dominant. For example, in copying a triangle, a perceptually dominant child can be seen tightly clutching his pencil, making sure it moves as requested, but perceiving only the tiniest fraction of a line at a time. The perception of the triangle as a whole form is not seen, nor can it be reproduced from memory. Learning visual perception is largely learning distortion, as in line perspective or a rotating disc. Interpretation of pictures in books and maps is almost entirely learned. Some primitive peoples or newly sighted people have similar learning problems with 2D representations.

Feedback. Children have to learn by exploration to monitor their own responses by the use of feedback in association with sensory perception. But to be effective in learning, sensory data of different kinds have to be co-ordinated and translated by the brain into meaning. A child without the ability for this co-ordination can perhaps read silently (visual behaviour); he can describe what he has read (auditory behaviour); but he cannot read aloud (auditory and visual behaviour together). The more primitive motor activity is the single form of feedback available.

Children with problems of co-ordinating their many perceptions at once often let one perceptual mode take the upper hand. It saves time and effort. Education has long recognised differences in learning styles between individuals, such as the auditory learner or the visual learner; but extreme dominance does slow down learning considerably.

The clumsy child. The medical term used for this exceedingly common cluster of problems in a child is – minimal brain dysfunction (MBD). Its prevalence ranges from 5 to 10 per cent of the population, depending on definition. It is not related to IQ. The effect on behaviour is only quantitively not qualitatively different to that of normal children, so that among normally active children playing outdoors they are not noticeable. But on a rainy day, or in the classroom, their extra activity and lack of movement control creates difficulties and emotional problems for themselves and others. The MBD child is described both at home and school as follows:

1 He has a short span of concentration. He does not watch TV or read a book for long. He only hears half an adult's instructions or sentences so that he can't remember even simple directions and cannot complete academic tasks.
2 He has difficulties in perceptual and cognitive functioning. He has difficulties in orientating objects in space, distinguishing right from left, auditory discrimination, short-term memory, arranging in sequence and generalising from one sense perception to another. Reading and writing problems are not uncommon.
3 He has problems with personal relationships. Such children tend to be impulsive, difficult to discipline and socialise. They cause damage and are difficult to toilet train. Although outgoing, they have few friends, tending to insist on their own rules.

Most MBD children are moody, 'short-fused' and prone to tears. Relationships between themselves and adults creep into unfortunate habits or irritation on the part of the adult, and feelings of low-esteem on the part of the child. Groups of peers and families tend to pick on the child and school performance is normally affected. Teacher comments such as – 'You're really quite bright, but you just aren't doing your best' – are deflating; when he *is*. One American study showed that MBD children made up about a half of adolescent underachievers.

Research on behaviour modification has been carried out in England with little benefit to report. Perhaps bio-feedback techniques would be effective. Drug therapy has been said to have remarkable results. Psychological therapy for the inevitable side-effects certainly helps, but is hard to get. The understanding, sympathetic schoolteacher is once more a problem child's source of comfort.

Learning handicaps. These are mostly the opposite of those benefits to learning described in Chapter 3, and the good effects of early social education as mentioned in Chapter 4.

These brakes on learning also include:

1 extreme poverty;
2 unfavourable social or cultural attitudes;
3 child neglect, or maltreatment;
4 personal problems in the child, probably arising from 1, 2, and 3, such as emotional deprivation;
5 extreme lack of stimulation;
6 specific physical handicaps, such as poor sight or hearing, which remain undiscovered or are neglected.

The teacher of young children is always in the 'crow's nest'. It is her responsibility and should be within her ability to bring to the notice of the appropriate welfare authorities any abnormalities which she feels need attention.

Dyslexia. This is a general term which covers the many varieties of reading disability. It is not a disease such that one might say – 'He's got dyslexia' – but it acts as a brake on learning of all sorts. It can arise from many causes both physical and psychological.

Reading problems start early for many of the reasons listed above. The earlier the identification the better the prognosis. Slow learning in other subjects at school can affect motivation and ability to read and vice versa. High anxiety is detrimental to school attainment including reading.

Treating reading disability and the inevitable psychological problems (before and after) would be most suitably done after a full investigation by a child guidance team. Ideally, every child should be screened for physical defects before reaching school. A child with, say, visual perception problems could then be taught appropriately from the start. At very least, different methods of teaching reading could be sorted out for the individual child. Where a blanket method, such as 'Look and Say', is applied to all the class, visually dyslexic children will be disadvantaged. This method teaches children to see words as wholes. Auditory dyslexics cannot distinguish between short vowel sounds and might spell 'cit' instead of 'cat'. Such a child would be confused by the 'phonic' method, which breaks up words in learning.

Were children to be screened for possible reading/learning difficulties, they could be sent to schools in which they could prosper, or receive beneficial remedial teaching from the start.

Remedial teaching puts considerable emphasis on repetition, which children in difficulties most often need. Screening is particularly important for the 'at risk' groups, such as those listed above and also those born into dyslexic families. Simple visual and auditory tests can be used by all teachers.

Behaviour therapy has been used successfully in some cases of reading difficulty. Another approach is to minimise distractions. The remedial teacher always has the difficult task of combining 'therapy' with an attack on the child's specific learning problems. An important means of success with reading problems is outlined on p. 87. In California recently, research work with children of very low intelligence showed that they could make up sentences with plastic symbols. This has followed similar work with chimpanzees. Perhaps similar 'concrete' methods of writing and reading can be devised for children with dyslexic problems from other causes. A coloured letter learning scheme has been devised; 'Words in Colour' obviously has drawbacks to the colour-blind, but is an effective method of teaching reading.

Help for the slow learner

Teaching the slow learner is a prime example of teaching to learn – in particularly difficult circumstances. The important parts of a slow learner's education (as is the case with other children) are the processes and not the product. In other words, how to set about the task, not what is achieved.

The type of dysfunction from which a child is suffering will be apparent in his learning behaviour. Normally, classrooms or groups function at a recognisable level. If a child has not reached that level of development, the teacher should be the first to notice, for the child will fail to reach the minimum goal of the lesson. Take, for example, a child set to colour-in a picture – 'He cannot colour the apple red, because he *cannot* find the apple. He is unable to differentiate the conflicting maze of lines he sees on the paper' (Kephart 1971). The task is meaningless, and this will show.

Tests. Various tests are issued for use by teachers. The Frostig Test of Visual Perception and the Illinois Test of Psycholinguistic Abilities are useful. But they would only be used when signs of learning problems have already been noted, and as an indication rather than a final conclusion. This can then give a clearer picture of the child's problems. Tests cannot predict with accuracy, at our present level of knowledge.

Slow development. As always, children should be educated according to their developmental level and not their chronological age. Children often vary in their developmental levels for different abilities. The teacher is frequently obliged to 'play it by ear'.

Disrupted development. Stages in development can be partially completed, or skipped entirely. Children will show this in their learning behaviour. The problem is to attempt to fill in the missing stages and the first move is to identify them. As each stage is dependent on the one before, a useful procedure is to go back through the stages till the disabled or missing one is reached. The teacher's task is then to mend the gap – to teach development. If the processes of learning are not mastered first, then the subject matter will never be understood.

Teaching such a child is extremely difficult and calls for particular teaching techniques, which may have to be evolved for the individual child. Children do not skip stages without cause, and it is not always possible for a teacher to find out what has gone wrong or how she may put it right. To add to the problem, life goes on. Although the child may be out of step and struggling, he is getting older and both home and school continue to make more complex demands on him. Thus, even when it is possible to fill a gap which appeared at age three, the child may now be six. The new teaching/learning techniques must be changed to accord with the present six-year-old pupil. To take away his devised learning props and ask him to perform at three-year-old level is to court deterioration in performance and lower morale.

Lateness of learning to read poses many such problems, since the reading material is so often meant for five-year-old minds. But new, simplified reading books are now being written for teenagers and adults who have 'missed the boat'.

Cases of extensive interference with development, spotted by the class teacher, are normally passed on to a specialist, such as a trained remedial teacher in the normal school, or a staff member of the child guidance clinic, or they are transferred to a special school. There are limits to what a normal schoolteacher is expected to be able to teach.

12
Maladjusted Children

Adjustment

Adjustment is not a static condition; this relationship between an individual and his environment varies, even from day to day. All adjustment is a learned behaviour, which is governed by the same principles that affect other forms of learning. But the degree of adjustment does itself affect other learning, such as school progress. A child is termed maladjusted when his adjustment is so poor that his unhappiness deflects his development from its expected route. Such children can show their condition in many ways – not necessarily in overt anti-social behaviour.

When a teacher is aware of the normal range of children's development and the various influences upon it, she will also be aware of the variations from it. Maladjusted behaviour is to some extent relative to the life-situation in which the pupil finds himself. The same behaviour may be tolerated in one situation and referred to the psychologist in another. Teachers, parents and doctors, sometimes in co-operation, most often are the people who make the decisions. Recent research has shown that teachers are as aware of the problems of the withdrawn child as they are of the disruptive child.

Behaviour disturbance is not confined to children. Adults in charge of children can cause terrible damage by their own maladjustment. Immaturity or mental disturbance in teachers can bring distress to both children and school staff, though stress and conflict in the classroom will affect each child differently. At present, though, it is difficult for local authorities, even if they are fully aware of an unhealthy situation of this kind, to do anything about it. In extreme cases, deputations of parents have sometimes resulted in a teacher's removal or obligatory 'rest'.

Identifying maladjustment

What is normal and what is abnormal behaviour depends on:

1 the individual concerned
2 the situation he is in, and
3 the consistency of the behaviour.

Everyone has moments of maladjustment, such as depression after 'flu or aggression due to fatigue or frustration. On the whole, they pass by without interference, so that potential maladjustment should be carefully watched before any action is taken. Many behaviour disorders, such as bed wetting or temper tantrums, are very common and to that extent 'normal'. Consequently, 'difficult' children, who are insolent, break the rules, bully other children, withdraw to unresponsiveness, lie, etc., may be crying for help. But they may also be behaving according to another set of rules, of their world outside school, which teachers with their socially orientated, middle-class values may have difficulty in understanding (p. 63).

It is possible that with knowledge and some sort of screening, maladjustment is detectable and manageable – before a child becomes delinquent. The recent development of quick questionnaires, which teachers can use either with suspect children or entire school populations, provides some scientific evidence. But as with many other aspects of child care, tests alone are insufficient. It is the sensitivity of the educator to spoken and unspoken communications between her and the child which begin the story.

Problem behaviour. A child's behaviour is considered to be a problem, not only when it is different from the normal pattern, but when it offends people's sense of propriety. Both adults and children judge each other; it is part of daily social inter-action. But some are more intolerant than others and some have more power to act than others. The gang of bullies in the playground has power over one small boy, which would be considered a problem – if adults ever found out. The teacher can be a destructive bully in the classroom too, of course, but her behaviour would probably be called 'strict' or 'eccentric'.

Children's behaviour must be individually evaluated in the context of the eternal triangle of home-school-child. Then, what is and what is not maladjusted behaviour may become clearer.

Home

The unhappy list of unpleasant circumstances on p. 108, in which many children are brought up, summarises the origins of what may result in maladjusted behaviour. Even in less dire circumstances, children can miss out on the basic psychological necessities and remain stunted or distorted in their development.

Emotional deprivation. Research work over decades has shown that children raised in situations such as old-style orphanages have not received sufficient affection to become loving and responsive themselves. The mother-baby bond has been given considerable attention in normal family life, although father's relationship to his baby has been largely ignored. But it is true that emotional deprivation in infants is followed by long-lasting and perhaps permanent ill-effect on personality – in particular, the ability to build relationships.

Emotional pressure. Parental demands, rigorously enforced, leave the child with the choice of complete compliance or rebellion. Excessive insistence on toilet training in infants can, for instance, result in the child withholding his faeces to produce constipation. The child then finds it even more difficult to perform, mother is more exasperated and an avoidable psychological *impasse* has resulted. The same type of parental behaviour can result in varieties of childhood rebellion – at any time of life. More rarely, such pressure does produce an over-obedient child. Such repressed children often find difficulties while growing up, such as in making friends of either sex, and eventually in taking on the responsibility of marriage and parenthood. Children under excessive pressure endure excessive anxiety. They build up personal defence mechanisms with which to cope with life. Other people may be surprised by the violence of the reaction when they inadvertently breach these defences.

Society. Socially acceptable (and thus adjusted) behaviour varies between families. But there is often a vast discrepancy between the ways of a minority sub-culture and those of the outside world. The child torn between a strongly enforced home culture and the culture of his school-mates can become seriously disturbed. The 'generation gap', that clash between the values of different age groups, is a well-known problem raiser of this kind.

Socially deprived children are handicapped in many ways, such as nutrition, intellectual stimulation, etc. They also have a higher than normal likelihood of physical and mental abnormality. In addition, they are frequently brought up on a regime of punishment. They do not feel that school and teachers are on the same wavelength as their outside experience and their education suffers. It is from this stratum of poor, educationally limited and discouraged children that most maladjusted and delinquent behaviour comes.

School

Control. Schools are themselves contributors to maladjustment in pupils. They are institutions which deliver values along with the information (see Chapter 5). The more control a school exerts, the less concern is usually shown for the individual pupil and his self-concept. Strict control appears to exist to promote learning, but can, beyond a minimum level, act against it. In order to be a good pupil, a child must submit to the rules of the school. But schools vary, so that the same behaviour in different schools may be punished or not; i.e. the level of expected subordination and initiative varies. Children who cannot accept the values of their school as relevant to their life experience may 'drop out', either mentally or physically, and will show their feelings in maladjusted behaviour.

Sensitivity. Teachers are not angels – favouritism and dislike are well-known in the classroom; their effects on children's self-image less so. One child may be picked on unknowingly by most of the staff in their different lessons. Probably no teacher has ever been to his home, so that none of them knows just how much mental battering he gets there too. Teachers can be purposefully and constantly unkind to pupils, with little regard for them as people, they may hold children up to ridicule, or deflate effort with sarcasm. If the learning experience is unpleasant, incomprehensible, boring or biased, children will (not illogically) under-achieve, hate the daily torment and misbehave.

Child

Growing up brings its own stresses, but some children are born with extra difficulties. Minimal brain dysfunction is difficult to detect, but may cause considerable disturbance. The study of genetic disorder still has a long way to go. Certain behaviour disorders occur at different times in the process of development. Judging by their frequency, what were once considered to be symptoms of maladjustment now appear to be a fairly normal part of growing up, such as occasional regression into an earlier stage of emotion, when the intellectual pressure is increased.

Adolescence. Although this is normally regarded as a turbulent time, much of the distress is due to adult attitudes in our Western world. For example, we *expect* adolescents to be troubled, if not troublesome. The increased length of dependence on adults as full-time education increases creates unnatural relationships and strains between the young adults and the older ones.

Emotional behaviour changes in adolescence:

1 it is notably more intense and spontaneous,
2 it can easily swing to extremes,

116

3 it is less easily controlled,
4 it can become over-controlled – as a 'mood'.

Sexual behaviour also changes, not only from maturation within the individual, but because certain patterns are expected to be followed. Parents of a seventeen-year-old girl do not expect her to prepare for her future, as they would a boy of the same age. Adolescent group conformity is well-known, although the all-American one-sex clique is less likely in Britain, especially among middle-class teenagers. However, the relative democracy of a friendship group, and where a teenager comes in its hierarchy, is important to his self-esteem and sense of identity.

As with other age groups, maladjustment in adolescents is relative. Often, what adults consider to be maladjustment is normal behaviour to the adolescent, or perhaps a readjustment to the spoken and unspoken demands of adult society.

Remedies

Understanding the causes of maladjustment goes a long way towards understanding how it may be prevented. But the logical measures which would follow call for deep-seated changes in administrative thinking, from government down. Home conditions come into the realm of the social welfare services (Freeman, 1968. Chapter 10), though many voluntary groups also play an essential part.

Some school conditions are more easily changeable at grass roots level. Reduction in teaching group size is often a matter of manoeuvring by staff, so that individual needs can be responded to. Teaching attitudes and ways of teaching can be changed, so that the school can render support where the home has failed, and perhaps prevent breakdown. Respect for children as people should always be a priority.

Teachers are a kind of parent substitute and some take this aspect of their task seriously. As teacher training changes, more teachers are coming into schools who see their work as considerably extended into a complex of social and intellectual skills. Some teachers qualify in counselling or act out their extended role by seeing children out of school, being a father-figure, etc. Teachers can be the bridges between home and school, where communication is otherwise lacking. Education is a social activity and the teacher its purveyor.

Training in social skills would be of particular value to teachers in difficult conditions. Carrying through observations means knowing where to get things done and how to understand and communicate with the social worker or other people whose help may be needed.

The morality put out by schools is often irrelevant to the pupils; moral education, or guidance in the form of discussion or otherwise, moved out of the religious education slot, is minimal at present. The aesthetically satisfying side of education is also given very short shrift in many primary and most secondary schools. Planning for leisure activities should be a notable part of education today.

When children are maladjusted and outside help is inadequate, it can help to isolate a small group of pupils from the rest of the class for part of the day. Even one disturbed child in a class can harass the teacher and disrupt school life considerably. His removal can be a surprising relief to both the teacher and the classroom atmosphere. Small children especially can find it easier to make contact with an adult and to adjust to school in a small group. Some head teachers see their obligations as helping a child to adjust, others as making him conform. School life and the behaviour of potentially or mildly maladjusted children hang on such attitudes.

13
Gifted Children

Recognition

Giftedness is what you choose it to be. Some American research has claimed as much as the top 30 per cent of the population as being gifted; British concern is generally with the top 2 per cent. But of what?

As with all ability, a child needs mental and physical nourishment. Where appropriate facilities are missing, so too are the gifted children. In this way, the prevalence of giftedness highlights the educational situation in different parts of the country. Assuming a roughly equal proportion of ability levels between different education authorities, one might ask why there are so few mathematicians in one, musicians in another, etc.; and whether the gifted gymnasts of one district are equal in ability to their neighbouring gifted gymnasts.

Children gifted in any way are normally conscious of their differences and, on the whole, children prefer to conform. Consequently, many gifted children are thought to hide their abilities at school and perform at a not too noticeable level. Being gifted, they are often very good at it. But the price of anonymity is high – frustration, boredom and disenchantment with school.

Gifts. Types of gifts must vary with the types of ability available for development. Gifts may be singular, in groups, or right across the board.

119

Studies of adult giftedness are virtually all retrospective and subject to the vagaries of anecdotal stories. Non-verbal concepts such as music and art are not normally considered to mature until adolescence. But some individuals, such as Mozart or Picasso, give evidence of very early development. Others, such as Leonard Bernstein or Van Gogh, developed late. If identifying giftedness were to be based on an idea of the early maturation of the growth sequence, then prediction would miss out the late developers. We do not know whether their particular abilities in childhood were different to those of their peers, nor do we know why some precocious children have failed to carry their promise into adulthood.

However, five main types of giftedness in children are suggested here:

(1) Intellectual. This is the easiest to measure, both in terms of infant development and with intelligence tests. High intelligence test scores (say 145 +) are not always on a par with high achievement in school. But it is usually only when parents protest about achievement levels, or when children misbehave, that these children of high potential ability are discovered. The gifted children who are better performers at conforming will remain 'average' at school.
(2) Technical. Primary schoolteachers can easily become dependent on the technically bright. The one who always puts up the model, whose work and understanding of the mechanics of things is outstanding, is invaluable in this situation.
(3) Aesthetic. In order to play an instrument, it is necessary to have access to it and in order to paint, one must have paper, paints and brushes. Brilliant sculptors may abound, for all we know, who have never seen a chisel. School aesthetics teaching is very varied in availability. Most aesthetically gifted children get that aspect of their education from home.
(4) Social. The socially gifted are particularly sensitive to other people and tend to be popular.
(5) Physical. The recent popularity of gymnastics has produced a number of highly talented gymnasts where there were none before. Physical gifts which could be used vocationally, such as football, have always been recognised. But the teaching of physical education as a whole seems to be expanding at present.

Enrichment. Education implies far more than the acquisition of knowledge, and the growing understanding of giftedness brings to schools yet another reason for 'enriching' education. Enriching the curriculum is important to all children, especially those from culturally poor homes. But it is of particular importance to children of potentially very high ability to have access to new modes of perception and to practise in many fields. Ability to play a violin, for instance, is particularly vulnerable to a late start. For all skills, the sooner the open mind and supple fingers of a young child begin to practise, the finer his perceptual and practical technique will become over time.

The development of high ability

Milestones

(1) Walking. Gifted children appear to walk at an earlier age than normal children. But the social-class differences on physical growth and development are important (Chapter 2).

(2) Talking. Girls seem to be more advanced than boys, but social-class differences have little effect. Although many gifted children speak earlier and more fluently than their contemporaries, it is not a sure sign of giftedness. Gesell suggests that such milestones are less important signs of intellectual gifts than early alertness, responsiveness and vocalisations.

(3) Reading. This ability is subject to many influences. Some gifted children teach themselves to read at three-years-old. But some may be prevented from doing so by parents, or lack of reading matter. Children can 'refuse' to read for psychological reasons. Girls tend to read earlier than boys.

(4) Cognitive development. Logical thinking, reasoning, mathematics and memory are considered together here. Many researchers have concluded that the gifted child is advanced in generalising ability (p. 34), that he has great ability to see relationships between objects and ideas and to apply them to new situations. The gifted child is likely to be in advance of other children in terms of Piaget's stages of development (see C2) and sometimes seems to jump stages. Such behaviour is confusing to teachers when, for instance, a child gets his sums right, but can't explain how he did it. He may also see ambi-

guities in questions which the rest of the class do not, causing him to pause before attempting the answer. This can even gain a child a reputation for slowness or awkwardness.

Arithmetical development is difficult to compare in children, as schools use different methods. Some schools drill their children on; others help them to individual discovery methods. Gifted child mathematicians often devise methods of their own, sometimes before they have reached school age.

The gifted child seems to have an exceptionally good memory from a very early age and brings it into use when gathering his store of knowledge. Teachers are most often able to accept good memory as a guide to giftedness.

Nursery, or very early educational provision, seems to be a most important influence on later school achievement. If a sample of gifted children is taken at age ten, it would probably be found that 60 per cent of them have had nursery education.

Other developmental indications

(1) Sleep. 'Problems' of children's sleep depend on what is expected by the parents. If children can read till they sleep, there are less likely to be 'problems' than if it's 'bed at six and lights out' for a child who needs less than twelve hours sleep. But for whatever reason, children most often noted as gifted seem to have more problems, or at least complaints, about their sleeping than the average.

(2) Physique. Every study on gifted children has concluded that they are above average height, weight, strength, etc. However, these physical indications of superiority are also tied to social-class attributes. Children discovered to be gifted do frequently come from the mentally and physically better off sections of society. It is possible, but unlikely, that late developers will catch up or take over (see Chapter 2 and Tanner, 1968).

(3) Health. Apart from the odd fact that short-sighted children appear to be brighter, gifted children are particularly healthy. It is possible that there is a high incidence of 'sensitivity' diseases, such as allergy or asthma, but again, an inclination to these troubles is found in children of the higher social classes.

(4) Friends. Gifted children are always children. Although some seek friends older than themselves, most are happiest among their own age group.

(5) Curiosity. Extreme and genuine curiosity is agreed by parents and teachers to be a sign of giftedness. Quality is important. Much asking of questions may merely be attention-seeking. Educators find this constant 'in-depth' questioning very wearing. But good, honest answering and solid data are vital to the gifted questioner. Teachers may be surprised to find that they have a tendency to answer some questions, or questioners, more readily than others by using a monitoring check-guide which they can devise themselves.

(6) Slow learners. The gifted child can suffer from any of the difficulties mentioned in Chapter 11, often giving the impression of stupidity. In addition, he may be impatient of the slow communication of his writing. His thoughts flow on too fast for his child's hand to keep up with and his writing and spelling are often terrible. Whether this is because of poor co-ordination or impatience is often hard to decide. Either way, writing and spelling achievement, exam conditions, etc., will mitigate against success in school. Many gifted children, given access to a typewriter, learn to use it with great happiness and at great speed, even though spelling may still be poor.

(7) Perception. Keen powers of perception are associated with giftedness, especially aesthetic perception. But teachers are not always aware of this ability in children, their own perception of children often getting in the way.

(8) Jigsaws. Gifted children are often amazingly good at and keen on doing jigsaws. They might serve as a useful identification tool.

(9) Energy. Gifted children are more intense bundles of energy than other children. It can be another problem to the adults around and may even be diagnosed as 'over-activity'. Extreme physical energy does make it difficult to sit still for long at school, and learning, in the formal school situation, may suffer. Boys have this 'problem' more than girls. As with many other childhood behaviours, 'bounce' in some situations may be labelled a 'problem'.

(10) Creativity (see p. 19). The creatively gifted child is as difficult to define as creativity itself. But by the use of the various means and expert judgements available, such children

can be identified in some spheres. The behaviour of creatively gifted children has been investigated, but almost all the research work has come under considerable criticism. Some creative gifts may take years to mature into recognition, while others may fade with childhood. Highly creative children are often said to have a well developed humour of the absurd.

Adjustment

It is here that the gifted child is likely to find problems, although most gifted children (as yet discovered) seem to be emotionally healthy. But again, tests of adjustment are somewhat affected by social-class attitudes and gifted children are generally middle-class.

Maladjustment in gifted children is sometimes due to an unbalanced growth of abilities. They can be unpopular and misbehave in class if they allow their brilliance full reign and be equally unpopular if they hold tight and make a poor attempt to be normal. The teacher may be as fooled as the pupils by this second approach. There is, as yet, only one school (boarding) in Britain which caters for the needs of gifted, maladjusted pupils.

Kellmer Pringle (1970), as part of her long follow-up study, found that among 'able misfits', too high or too low parental expectations often contributed to the child's maladjustment. 'Atypical family situations', unhappy homes, illogical parental discipline and 'inconsistent handling' occurred more in this group than in the population at large. It is suggested that 'good intellectual ability by itself is insufficient to compensate for inadequate parental support and interest'.

Kellmer Pringle also found that her 'able misfits' were given less than average opportunity for gaining independence, though more boys than girls were given such opportunities. Parental attitudes were the most important factors in allowing children their outlets. However, extraordinary initiative, extreme independence, the ability to work alone and self-confidence are seen by all researchers as important facets of the gifted child's personality.

Parents and teachers can feel threatened by a child who seems to know far more than they do, or they may allow him to 'take over' the family or class. He is thus presented with situations with which he may not be emotionally able to cope. Relationships of everyone concerned will then be likely to suffer.

Although gifted children most often perceive themselves as different, it rarely seems to bother them. But because such children can occupy themselves alone for hours, they appear to be introverted and thus, by logic, 'unhappy'. Their apparent fondness for daydreaming and dislike of large groups adds to this image of the sad and alone child.

Education

Gifted children are very often bored at school. Like the slow learner, the child is either doomed to hours of boredom in a formal school situation, or he will look round for relief in the form of more challenging problems and may become a ring-leader in mischief.

It is hard for the teacher to keep a gifted child 'stretched' and able to achieve his potential in the normal school situation. But even with supreme effort from his teacher, a child's achievement will still be relative to the school and home conditions he experiences. Two children of the same high IQ can perform quite differently in public examinations, depending on their circumstances. Kellmer Pringle found that able children who achieved less than they were capable of had 'a high incidence of emotional difficulties'. The teachers of her able sample thought of their pupils as of average or below normal ability. They seemed to judge ability mostly on achievement, as other researchers have found. Thus, a bright under-achiever is likely to remain unrecognised, setting up a vicious circle leading to maladjustment.

How to educate the gifted is the subject of debate. Some would remove them from normal children and educate them in special schools; others would have special provision made for them in the normal situation. Tempest (1974) outlines what was attempted in a four-year experiment of separating off gifted children into a special class, yet leaving them in the normal school. Their teacher devised a special programme for this super stream. The results are still being followed up, but

125

the book contains interesting educational ideas. Bridges' (1973) book looks sympathetically at the problems of the gifted child in the normal school. He comes up with other ideas, such as bussing them round, like a football team, to places of further educational interest.

Advancing children a form or two to keep up with their intellectual level has its difficulties. Younger children get out of their emotional depth; teachers forget how young they are and make no allowance; classmates can be jealous or can't be bothered with the younger child. It is not easy to have an 'old' mind in a young body.

Needs

Love. Gifted children are still children; they need at least as much affection and reassurance as a normal child and often receive less. This is due to their behaviour, such as apparent maturity and competence or an over-demand for attention, resulting in irritation. But, when the violin is finally put back in its case after a three-hour session, perhaps teddy and bedtime attention are even more important. Parents and teachers sometimes seem to hover between a strong desire to make the difficult child conform, and simply giving up as educators, in case they get in the way of something wonderful.

Gifted children of any disposition need *challenge* rather than spoon-feeding. Teachers and parents may find themselves more in the position of a testing board or assault course for a child's fertile imagination, than in more conventional roles. Children of high ability have a lot to offer the world – too much is still running to waste.

14
Educational Psychology in Practice

Educational psychology today is concerned with the early detection of problems in children and with possible preventive measures which authorities might take. It is effective both in and out of school life. The service includes advice and treatment for all children (whether normal or handicapped) who may require these.

The educational psychologist

Training. An educational psychologist first obtains an honours degree in psychology or its equivalent. She must have at least two years teaching experience before being accepted for further training. This is usually a one-year course, which ends with examinations and the presentation of a dissertation of original research. The successful psychologist is then awarded a Diploma in Educational Psychology or, more recently, a Master's degree. The time taken to reach this goal is at least seven years and often more.

Relationships with schools. It is important for the psychologist to be able to understand and to work within the framework of the education system. But in spite of the obligatory teaching certificate and teaching experience, there is sometimes a little discord between psychologists and teachers. For instance, psychologists complain that teachers don't read and take note of their reports; teachers say they can't understand the jargon! Unless there is real communication, the best work, conducted even in ideal circumstances, can be a waste of time and effort.

The psychological report. The psychologist can vary the style of her report, depending on whom she expects to read it. Most often, several people – teachers, doctors, social workers, even parents – will have access to it. Consequently, the psychologist tends to compromise and write a brief report. This will probably include an account of:

1 the child's level of interest and co-operation in the test situation;
2 names and possibly descriptions of the tests used;
3 any special circumstances liable to affect the reliability of the results;
4 some general conclusions;
5 recommendations and suggestions for education and/or treatment of the child.

Test results in figures, such as IQ scores, are not always given. This is because they can be misleading, since those who may read it cannot always be familiar with the specific tests used. Instead, the psychologist often gives the child's scores in terms of a range, within which the child appears to fit. Intelligence could be said to be 'good/average', for instance. Some psychologists write two reports. One is precise and technical, saying what has been done and with what results; the other is brief and is suitable for more general use.

Communication with parents. Depending on the psychologist, parents sometimes sit in at the testing session. A good psychologist does her utmost to explain what is going to happen, so that parents can co-operate. Otherwise, interference in the form of – 'He's never played with that kind of toy before' – can be disruptive.

Parents can be excellent observers of their children and thus immensely valuable sources of information about a child's daily life. There is normally some bias in a parent's report, but it is an acceptable principle that parents' observations of their child's present behaviour are notably more reliable than their anecdotal memories of what happened in the past.

128

Education and psychology are both becoming somewhat more friendly towards parents. In the same way as they are beginning to operate in the daily life of the more open schools, they are being asked to help in the treatment of their child. 'Parent guidance', i.e. teaching parents how to guide, has been practised in the treatment of deaf babies for many years. It is now being used in the treatment of autistic, sub-normal or otherwise handicapped children. As parents' attitudes and home background are undoubtedly the most important influences on a child's life, then their co-operation would seem to be essential.

It is not always easy to bring or keep parents in touch with either teaching methods or psychological treatment. Specially trained staff, such as school counsellors or educational social workers, are of great value in that respect, but teachers and psychologists are equally capable of making contact and thereby gaining greater insight themselves.

Involving parents with their children's out-of-home lives is almost always beneficial to the child. It is particularly valuable if this involvement begins before a child goes to school. Early diagnosis of educational problems is the quickest route to their solution. Psychologists and teachers are very well placed to help parents to help their children in the use of toys, activities, etc. The psychologist works at three levels in this respect (Mittler, 1970):

1 Knowledge of general child development enables the psychologist to plan suitable activities to improve a child's performance.
2 Professional skills of identifying an individual child's abilities in some detail enables the psychologist to be precise in planning activities.
3 The psychologist can collaborate with teachers and therapists in designing a remedial programme, which will be based, to some extent, on her detailed findings.

The child. Sometimes, the most important person in the plot is not even consulted. Even very young children can be capable of understanding what is going on. Parents who spring the child guidance clinic and the psychologist who goes along with this arrangement as a surprise are not doing their best for the child. 'Just do the puzzles and be good' is a common, but unfortunate, attitude that adults show to children.

However, whatever attitudes adults choose to have, children will form their own. A relationship between a child and an adult which is founded on truth and mutual respect is always more beneficial to both. A 'friendly' psychologist who tries to mislead a child for apparently professional purposes is less effective than one who explains what he is doing and why; the same goes for the results. But the explanation must obviously be appropriate. Children at home and at school are constantly being informed of their 'failures' and 'successes'; the educational psychologist has a far more informed basis from which to communicate and need not feel 'unprofessional' in doing so.

Children are always individuals. Although teachers and psychologists find it more convenient to diagnose and categorise, it is a destructive measure for many children. 'Poor learners' or 'school leavers' are categories, not children. The stereotyped models on which all professional educators must draw from time to time have their side-effects. No specific condition, such as poor writing, has the identical causes and results in any two children. Educators who use stereotypes inevitably make assumptions about cause and effect which are not necessarily justifiable. An example might be financial poverty and poor reading ability; if the two are wrongly assumed to be related, then the remedial programme is unlikely to be effective.

The psychological service

This is officially divided into two:

1 the child guidance clinic,
2 the schools psychological service.

But in practice, the structure of the service varies between local authorities. Psychologists can play one role or both; they can have a light work load or an impossible one; secretarial help or none. Their working conditions have, of course, a significant effect on what they can do. Teachers are not always aware of the type of set-up in their own area. In most areas, educational psychologists are not able to specialise but work as a member of the child guidance team, as well as in the school psychological service. In larger authorities, some may specialise in different aspects of educational psychology, such as severe subnormality or physically handicapped children.

The child guidance clinic. This is the headquarters of the child guidance service. Its main functions are the diagnosis and treatment of children's psychological disturbances and developmental difficulties. It copes (so far as it can) with any children whose condition requires psychological or psychiatric therapy.

The team usually consists of:

child psychiatrists
educational psychologists
psychiatric social workers.

Treatment is normally carried out under the direction of the child psychiatrist, who, as medical director of the clinic, determines its scope and nature. Psychiatrists are medical doctors who have taken post-graduate training in the speciality of mental illness. Their function is to be therapeutic, i.e. to help to cure.

The psychologist's role in the clinic is to report on the whole child – his abilities and the uses he makes of them, his behaviour and his self-concept. The psychologist has to discuss the child with the school, preferably on a visit, though this is not always possible. Once the clinic team have decided what is wrong with a child and what they are going to do, it is the psychologist's responsibility to keep communication flowing between the clinic and the school. In many instances, the active co-operation of the child's teachers will be a necessary part of the treatment. The psychologist, as interpreter, must know just what is practicable in the schools in her area.

The psychiatric social worker is the clinic's liaison with the home. She visits parents and it is on her skill at making relationships that much of the success of the child's treatment depends. Occasionally, children are referred to clinic over the parents' heads, by schools or doctors. The surprised and resentful parents then become the social worker's concern.

Some teams also employ a psychotherapist. She is also a psychologist, but is more concerned with treatment than reporting. She has training in the handling and interpretation of children's play and behaviour, in such a way as to help them to reach psychological health. The psychotherapist usually comes into the picture when the other team members have made their decisions. She usually treats cases needing longer and more intensive treatment. It is only right to say that child guidance facilities are very inadequate in most areas and there may be long delays before a child can even be seen for diagnosis.

The schools psychological service. This has responsibilities to education officers and teachers and is directed by a psychologist. Its aim is to contribute to the healthy development of children through the application of psychological knowledge to education.

School psychologists work in an advisory capacity and also with individual children. They contribute to general educational policy, school transfer arrangements, placement of handicapped pupils, courses for teachers and social workers, contributions to teaching approaches, local research and so on. These involve close co-operation with educational officers, school medical officers and head and assistant teachers.

The school psychologist acts as a consultant and can also carry out special studies for teachers and others. She may help to form the programme for remedial education or take part in it directly. She helps and advises schools and parents and may recommend referral to the child guidance clinic for particular cases.

It is the psychologist's dual role to be able to speak the same 'language' as the teacher and the clinic. Teaching is her concern as much as treatment and she is able to suggest specific practices to both in their own terms. But child guidance rarely produces dramatic changes in children's behaviour in a short time. The children concerned have often been damaged over a long period; short sharp cures are suspect and rare.

Direct referrals of children from school to psychologist are the quickest way of obtaining help for children. The psychologist's office is normally in the clinic. Copies of all psychological reports on children are sent to the divisional education office, as well as the schools concerned. Teachers can ask for more precise details of the services that their own local psychological set-up offers.

The remedial teaching service

In general, this exists to meet three types of need:

1 Children of below average ability, who are backward in one or more of the basic school subjects.
2 Children of above average ability, who are not achieving their potential. They are often grouped in 'opportunity' classes, where the problem does not loom large. For example, poor readers can learn to read without obviously attending a reading lesson.
3 Children with emotional disturbance in junior schools should be taught in groups of not more than six. The educational psychologist is involved with the decisions of who enters the groups and what is taught there. Remedial teachers do work on their own sometimes, or in association with the educational psychologist.

Child therapy

Children with problems affect their teachers and contribute to the unhappy atmosphere in some schools. The normal solution is to diagnose and treat the problem very much on the medical model (see F3 and F8). Child and parent (often only the mother) attend a clinic once a week for a fifty-minute session. When they are too troublesome for a normal school, children are deemed maladjusted or subnormal and sent to a special school. It is possible that this course seems to alienate the child; and certainly immigrant groups, who are over-represented in these schools, are distressed.

Large-scale research on the Isle of Wight gave a conservative estimate that 10 per cent of all children need psychological help. Were only a quarter of these to be treated, all the psychologists and special schools together would be insufficient. There is clearly a need for more people involved with children to take on more of the therapeutic role. Not only school counsellors and social workers, but classroom teachers have the ability to ease children's educational problems. The need is especially urgent in depressed areas, but it takes money to re-train and to keep the staff-pupil ratio low.

133

Types of therapy. An individual psychologist or psychiatrist will be drawn by his own personal feelings towards a balance between an entirely physical approach and a purely psychological one. The spectrum of types of therapy available is long (Varma, 1974) and varies from the conditioned reflex of behaviour therapy to different types of psychoanalysis (see F3).

The treatment of family units as a whole is receiving more attention of late and the growth of sensitivity groups, at least among young adults, suggests promising varieties of therapy. Group therapy or brief forms of one-to-one psychotherapy are valuable for the under-served, troubled adolescent. Teachers who wish to become better acquainted with forms of therapy, but without additional formal training, find that participation in such groups themselves is a great mind-opener.

Conclusions

An essential part of learning about applied psychology in education is that the teacher knows she is not isolated. She is aware of her role alongside the school psychological services, the welfare services and other environmental influences which reinforce or contradict school learning.

The teacher who is confident in what she is attempting to do is not isolated from the community. Assistants, as well as head teachers, are able to throw open their teaching areas to parents and visitors, without the feeling of invaded privacy. What, after all, is a school concealing by only inviting parents in two or three times a year? Parents, expert or not, are a valuable source of information to all the school.

Psychological education, as part of a child's development, is a primary process of opening minds. The child who is aware of his own developmental growth, and what he might expect, is in a far more confident position than he would otherwise be. Children in schools should be aware of their education within a wider frame of reference.

Education is broader without the artificial barriers of what is, and what is not, separate parts of a separate school curriculum. Learning always involves selection and, to a certain extent, coding or categorisation. A considerable amount of experience and information is normally discarded because it is of no obvious use to the learner at that moment. We have not yet discovered a method of total mental absorption, but considerable knowledge of mental processing allows education-alists to be aware of methods by which children can be taught to help themselves to what is around them.

Developmental psychology is not a new study; but careful scientific research, rather than anecdotal reminiscence, belongs to this century. But most teachers still leave their courses without sound statistical knowledge and ability to read and criticise educational research at first hand. Improvement in this field is vital to progress.

Assessment is of particular importance to teachers, but again relatively few teachers learn how to use the tools of the trade. Being able to assess a child's development and progress is a part of everyday teaching, but is largely practised without scientific technique. Psychology is not precise and reliable, it probably never will be, but even now there are sufficiently manageable techniques available which can greatly improve the processes of education.

Children's development is open to influence of all kinds. The 'deschoolers' would rather the schools kept out of it. But, at least for the moment, there is no more concentrated source of educational energy from which light might shine. Whatever the previous (and sometimes present), repressive functions of schools may have been, there is now considerable pressure to open out education, based on the understandings of develop-mental psychology. Child-centred education is focused on the individual child; it implies the growth of a human being, rather than the production of a cog to fit the system.

Objections are inevitable when education changes. 'If you teach all the children to read, who will work the looms?' 'They only play at school, nowadays'. 'Schools are failing to teach discipline'. Teaching is a part of society as a whole; it is con-siderably influenced by the prevailing wind of what is done, rather than what individuals feel *ought* to be done.

Yet, education is to some extent well ahead of public opinion by virtue of the knowledge of developmental psy-chology, and concern for each child. Were such knowledge to be universally applied by teachers acting partly as psycholo-gists, education could easily be freed from the mental cages of the people who teach, and their imposition on the people who learn.

Recommended Reading

Part I

Butcher, H. J. (1968) *Human Intelligence*. London: Methuen.

Buzan, Tony (1974) *Use Your Head*. London: BBC Publications.

Cashdan, A. and Whitehead, J. (eds.) (1971) *Personality Growth and Learning*. (Open University set book) London: Faculty of Educational Studies.

Danziger, K. (1971) *Socialisation*. Harmondsworth: Penguin.

Dean, Joan and Nichols, Ruth (1974) *Framework for Reading*. London: Evans Brothers.

Freeman, Joan (1968) *Human Biology and Hygiene*. Oxford: Pergamon Press.

Handley, George D. (1973) *Personality Learning and Teaching*. London: R. K. P. Students Library of Education.

Tanner, J. M. (1968) *Education and Physical Growth*. London: University of London Press.

Tough, Joan (1973) *Focus on Meaning*. London: George Allen & Unwin.

Part II

Cohen, A. and Garner, V. (1963) *A Students' Guide to Teaching Practice*. University of London Press.

Craft, M., Raynor, J. and Cohen, L. (1967) *Linking Home and School*. London: Longmans.

Hopson, Barrie and Hayes, John (1968) *The Theory and Practice of Vocational Guidance*. Oxford: Pergamon.

Hudson, B. (1973) *Assessment Techniques*. London: Methuen.

Morrison, A. and McIntyre, D. (1969) *Teachers and Teaching*. Harmondsworth: Penguin Books.

Moully, George J. (1960) *Psychology for Effective Teaching*. New York: Holt, Rinehart & Winston.

Stefflre, B. (ed.) (1965) *Theories of Counselling*. New York: McGraw Hill.

Stones, E. (1966) *Educational Psychology*. London: Methuen.

Stones, E. and Anderson, D. (1972) *Educational Objectives and the Teaching of Educational Psychology*. London: Methuen.

Part III

Bridges, S. (1973) *I.Q. 150*. London: Priory Press Ltd.

Kephart, Newell C. (1971) *The Slow Learner in the Classroom*. Ohio: Charles E. Merrill.

Segal, S. S. (1967) *No Child is Ineducable*. Oxford: Pergamon.

Tempest, N. R. (1974) *Teaching Clever Children*. London: RKP.

Varma, Ved P. (1973) *Stresses in Children*. University of London Press.

Varma, Ved P. (1974) *Psychotherapy Today*. London: Constable.

Williams, Phillip (1974) *Behaviour Problems in School*. University of London Press.

References
and Name Index

(The numbers in italics following each reference refer to page numbers within this book.)

Bernstein, Basil (1960) Language and Social Class. *British Journal of Sociology*, 271–6. *24, 40*

Bowlby, John (1951) Maternal Care and Mental Health. *Bull. Wld. Health Org. 3*, 357. *23*

Bridges, S. (1973) *I.Q. 150*. London: Priory Press. *126*

Burt, C. (1940) *The Factors of the Mind*. University of London Press. *15*

Bygrave, Mike, Goodman, Joan and Fordham, John (1973) *The Others Careers*. London: Wildwood House. *100*

Cattell, R. B. (1965) *The Scientific Basis of Personality*. London: Penguin. *16*

Douglas, J. B. W. (1964) *The Home and School*. London: McGibbon and Kee. *39, 54*

Douglas, J. B. W. (1968) *All our Future*. London: Peter Davies. *39, 44*

Erikson, E. H. (1965) *Childhood and Society*. Harmondsworth: Penguin. *44*

Eysenck, H. J. (1971) *Race, Intelligence and Education*. London: Temple Smith. *13*

Gesell, Arnold (1950) *The First Five Years of Life*. London: Methuen. *22, 121*

Guilford, J. P. (1967) *The Nature of Human Intelligence*. New York: McGraw Hill. *16*

Handley, George D. (1973) *Personality Learning and Teaching*. London: R. K. P. Students Library of Education. *46*

Harlow, H. F. (June 1959) Love in infant monkeys. *Scientific*

American (offprint 429). Obtainable from W. F. Freeman and Co., London. *23*

Hess and Shipman in A. Cashdan and J. Whitehead (eds.) (1971) *Personality, Growth and Learning.* (Open University set book) London: Faculty of Educational Studies. *89*

Jensen, Arthur R. (1972) *Genetics and Education.* London: Methuen. *13*

Kellmer-Pringle, Mia L. (1970) *Able Misfits.* London: Longman. *125*

Kephart, Newall C. (1971) *The Slow Learner in the Classroom.* Ohio: Charles E. Merrill. *106, 109*

Lawrence, D. (1973) *Improved Reading Through Counselling.* London: Ward Lock Educational. *87*

McClelland, D. A. (ed.) (1953) *The Achievement Motive.* New York: Appleton-Crofts. *42*

Mittler, Peter (ed.) (1970) *The Psychological Assessment of Mental and Physical Handicaps.* London: Methuen. *129*

Morrison, A. and McIntyre, D. (1969) *Teachers and Teaching.* Harmondsworth: Penguin Books. *78*

Mussen, P. H., Conger, J. J. and Kagan, J. (1965) *Child Development and Personality.* New York: Harper and Row. *44*

Newson, J. and Newson, E. (1963) *Four Years Old in an Urban Community.* London: Allen and Unwin. *40*

Piaget, J. (1932) *The Moral Judgement of the Child.* London: R. K. P. and (1953) *The Origins of Intelligence in the Child.* London: R. K. P. *16, 41, 51*

Piaget, J. and Inhelder, B. (1958) *The Growth of Logical Thinking from Childhood to Adolescence.* London: R. K. P. *29*

Rogers, C. in B. Stefflre (ed.) (1965) *Theories of Counselling.* New York: McGraw Hill. *91*

Skinner, B. F. (1953) *Science and Human Behaviour.* New York: Macmillan. *71*

Stones, E. (1970) *Readings in Educational Psychology.* London: Methuen. *74*

Tanner, J. M. (1968) *Education and Physical Growth.* University of London Press. *29, 122*

Tempest, N. R. (1974) *Teaching Clever Children.* London: R. K. P. *125*

Tough, Joan (1973) *Focus on Meaning.* London: George Allen and Unwin. *89*

Varma, Ved P. (1974) *Psychotherapy Today.* London: Constable. *134*

Subject Index

142